cakes and loaves

Ilona Chovancova
Photography by Pierre Javelle

# cakes and loaves

110 recipes you can make at home

whitecap

# INTRODUCTION

ARE YOU LOOKING FOR A BIT OF VARIETY IN YOUR USUAL MEALS? LOOK NO FURTHER — THIS BOOK IS HERE TO HELP. ALL THE RECIPES ARE BOTH SPEEDY AND EASY. SO, WHAT DO YOU HAVE TO DO? JUST BREAK, BEAT, MIX, AND SEASON. THAT IS IT — WELL, ALMOST... YOU WILL HAVE TO BAKE THE CAKES TOO, OF COURSE. WHAT WILL YOU NEED? A FEW EGGS, A LITTLE OIL OR BUTTER, SOME MILK AND FLOUR, AND A SPRINKLING OF SPICES OR FRESH HERBS. JUST MIX THEM ALL UP, AROUND AND IN, POP THE RESULT IN THE OVEN, AND VOILA!

HOW AND WHEN DO YOU SERVE THE CAKES? HOT, WARM, OR COLD? IN THE MORNING, AT MIDDAY, OR IN THE EVENING? IT IS ENTIRELY UP TO YOU. A CAKE MADE WITH WHOLE-WHEAT FLOUR AND SERVED WITH JAM IS A PERFECT REPLACEMENT FOR BREAD AT BREAKFAST. AT LUNCHTIME YOU CAN ENJOY A QUICK SANDWICH MADE WITH SLICES OF SAVORY CAKE. SERVE IT WITH A SALAD FOR SUPPER OR IN SMALL CHUNKS WITH AN APERITIF.

BE CREATIVE. FIND AN INGREDIENT YOU LIKE, ADD ANOTHER, AND YOU HAVE GOT A GREAT CAKE ON YOUR HANDS.

ALL I NEED TO SAY NOW IS: GET BAKING, GET TASTING, AND ENJOY!

ILONA

# * GETTING STARTED *

# THE RIGHT TOOLS

YOU DON'T REQUIRE SPECIAL SKILLS OR EQUIPMENT TO MAKE GOOD CAKES BUT IT IS DEFINITELY WORTH HAVING A FEW BASICS.

## CHECKLIST

Before beginning any recipe, be sure to have all of the following:

• a large mixing bowl

• a whisk to beat eggs (a food processor is great for some tasks but not essential)

• a wooden mixing spoon for beating, a metal tablespoon for folding, and a spatula for scraping the bowl

• a grater, for making cakes that contain grated fruit or vegetables

• a set of scales

• and, of course, a cake pan (your choice of shape)

## BAKING PAPER

Lining the pan with baking paper ensures that nothing sticks to it. To be sure the paper sticks properly to the pan, crinkle it up before using and dampen the inside of the pan lightly.

## MORTAR AND PESTLE

This is the must-have tool in my kitchen. I use mine for coarsely grinding nuts, chocolate, and cookies as well as for grinding spices such as coriander seed, aniseed, cloves, and cardamom pods. It is also useful when preparing pesto or other herb-based sauces.

## CAKE PANS

These days, there are so many different types of pan to choose from, in various shapes and sizes, some solid, some with removable bases, and in a variety of materials: silicone, non-stick, aluminum. A rectangular pan works well for a classic loaf cake, a large pan for something festive, or small ones for individual portions.

## PREPARING THE PAN

No matter what kind of pan you use, it must be prepared before you add the batter to prevent the cake from sticking when you turn out it.

### Silicone pans

These are the most practical kind of pans, and the easiest to use. Moisten a piece of paper towel with some oil and rub this around the insides of the mold and it is ready to use. Rest assured that your cake will come out of the pan very easily. To keep them clean, be sure to wash by hand and not in the dishwasher otherwise they will lose their non-stick capacity.

### Non-stick pans

If the coating is in good condition, without too many scratches, then you need only rub it with some butter or oil. However, if you are preparing sweet cakes, you should grease the surface and dust lightly with flour to prevent the cake from sticking. Otherwise, you will find it difficult to turn out the cake.

### Aluminum pans

This kind of pan must be greased and dusted with flour before baking.

### Individual pans

This shape is ideal for picnics, parties, or for children's cakes.

# BAKING, TURNING OUT, AND STORING

## BAKING

All cooking times have been tested using an electric oven; as a rule of thumb, allow 50 minutes for savory cakes and 40 minutes for sweet cakes.

If you are using a convection oven, cooking time should be reduced by half.

If you use individual pans, the cooking time should be reduced; allow 20–25 minutes.

If the cake browns too quickly during cooking, protect it by covering the pan with a sheet of aluminum foil.

## TESTING FOR DONENESS

I highly recommend keeping a supply of thin wooden skewers on hand for this task. Simply insert the skewer into the middle of the cake; if it comes out clean, the cake is done. Remove from the oven and let cool before turning out. If the batter seems thin and is still sticking to the skewer, continue baking for a few minutes longer. The tip of a knife can also be used to test doneness.

## MY TECHNIQUE FOR TURNING OUT

### For savory cakes

Before turning out a savory cake, be sure it is completely cooled. This will prevent the cake from splitting. If you are using aluminum or non-stick pans, run the edge of a knife around the inside of the pan before inverting it.

### For sweet cakes

It is easier to turn out a sweet cake while it is still slightly warm, unless you are using a silicone mold. If you are using aluminum or non-stick pans, run the edge of a knife around the inside of the pan before inverting it.

## STORING THE CAKE

This is only a problem when you have any cake left, which doesn't often happen. Most cakes can be stored for up to three days in the refrigerator. Remove about 30 minutes ahead to return the cake to room temperature before serving.

# FLOUR POWER

I USE CAKE FLOUR FOR MOST OF MY BAKING AS
THIS TYPE HAS THE LOWEST GLUTEN CONTENT.
IT ENSURES THE FINISHED PRODUCT WILL BE
LIGHT AND FLUFFY.

I ALSO LIKE TO MIX FLOUR TYPES WHEN
BAKING TO ACHIEVE DIFFERENT RESULTS.

## WHOLE-WHEAT FLOUR

This is made from whole grains and is rich in
fiber. It can be used to replace ordinary flour
but the cake will be darker in color and have a
stronger taste.

## CHESTNUT FLOUR

This is slightly sweet and results in cakes that
are darker in color. Allow one-third chestnut flour
to two-thirds cake flour in recipes.

## BUCKWHEAT FLOUR

Made from buckwheat, this flour contains no
gluten and does not rise in baking, so it should
be mixed with cake flour.

## RYE FLOUR

This does not contain any gluten. It is often used
for breads and spice cakes. It lends a slightly sticky
and chewy texture to cakes so it is always best to
use in conjunction with cake flour.

## CORNMEAL OR FINE GRADE POLENTA

This is very low in gluten so does not help cakes to
rise; once again, you need to mix it with cake flour
in your baking. It lends a pretty yellow color to
finished cakes.

All of the flour types can be found in
supermarkets, either in the baking section or the
health food aisles, or in health food stores.

CHICKEN AND CURRY CAKE * CARROT AND ZUCCHINI

AND CURED HAM CAKE * TWO-OLIVE CAKE * EGGF

ZUCCHINI AND BLACK SESAME SEED * BEET, MOZZ

CAKE * SPINACH AND GARBANZO BEAN CAKE * AF

SORREL CAKE * BELL PEPPER AND CUMIN CAKE * Z

CAKE * PARSNIP AND THYME * ITALIAN CAKE * GREE

CHICKEN DILL CAKE * CHERRY TOMATO, SHALLOT, AN

AND CHILI CAKE * ROASTED VEGETABLE CAKE

CAKE * FETA CHEESE AND HERB * CHICKEN AND CU

* ROQUEFORT CAKE * FIG AND CURED HAM C

CAKE * PUMPKIN AND CHILI CAKE * ZUCCHINI AND

* WATERCRESS AND SWEET POTATO CAKE * SPINACH

MUSTARD CAKE * SHRIMP AND SORREL CAKE * BELL

* MUSHROOM AND PARSLEY CAKE * PARSNIP AND TH

DRIED TOMATOES * SMOKED CHICKEN DILL C

* PARSLEY AND CHILI CAKE * ROASTED VEGETABLE

AND CELERY CAKE * FETA CHEESE AND HERB * CHI

* BEER CAKE * ROQUEFORT CAKE * FIG AND CURED

CAKE * PUMPKIN AND CHILI CAKE * ZUCCHINI

LIME * WATERCRESS AND SWEET POTATO CAKE *

HORSERADISH * MUSTARD CAKE * SHRIMP AND SORR

AND PARMESAN * MUSHROOM AND PARSLEY CAKE * P

FETA, AND SUN-DRIED TOMATOES * SMOKED CHI

CAKE * BEER CAKE * ROQUEFORT CAKE * FI

NT AND MINT CAKE * PUMPKIN AND CHILI CAKE

ELLA, AND LIME * WATERCRESS AND SWEET POTAT

E AND HORSERADISH * MUSTARD CAKE * SHRIMP AN

CCHINI AND PARMESAN * MUSHROOM AND PARSLE

BEANS, FETA, AND SUN-DRIED TOMATOES * SMOKE

CILANTRO CAKE * SAVORY CAKES * PARSLE

PARMESAN CHEESE CAKE * CHESTNUT AND CELER

Y CAKE * CARROT AND ZUCCHINI CAKE * BEER CAK

E * TWO-OLIVE CAKE * EGGPLANT AND MIN

ACK SESAME SEED * BEET, MOZZARELLA, AND LIM

ND GARBANZO BEAN CAKE * APPLE AND HORSERADIS

EPPER AND CUMIN CAKE * ZUCCHINI AND PARMESA

E * ITALIAN CAKE * GREEN BEANS, FETA, AND SUN

E * CHERRY TOMATO, SHALLOT, AND CILANTRO CAK

AKE * PARMESAN CHEESE CAKE * CHESTNUT

EN AND CURRY CAKE * CARROT AND ZUCCHINI CAK

M CAKE * TWO-OLIVE CAKE * EGGPLANT AND MINT

D BLACK SESAME SEED * BEET, MOZZARELLA, AN

PINACH AND GARBANZO BEAN CAKE * APPLE AN

CAKE * BELL PEPPER AND CUMIN CAKE * ZUCCHIN

SNIP AND THYME * ITALIAN CAKE * GREEN BEANS

EN DILL CAKE * CHERRY TOMATO, SHALLOT, AN

# CREATING YOUR OWN RECIPES

AS EVERYONE KNOWS, IT IS VERY SATISFYING WHEN BAKING TO MAKE A CAKE THAT IS ORIGINAL AND REFLECTS YOUR PERSONAL PREFERENCES. HERE ARE SOME IDEAS TO HELP YOU CREATE YOUR OWN CAKE RECIPES, BUT YOU CAN ADAPT THEM ACCORDING TO YOUR OWN TASTE. JUST BE SURE THAT THE TOTAL WEIGHT OF INGREDIENTS ADDED TO THE BASIC RECIPE DOES NOT EXCEED 10 OZ (300 G).

## BASIC RECIPE

Preparation time: 15 minutes
Cooking time: 50 minutes

**3 eggs**
**6 Tbsp (3½ fl oz/100 mL) low-fat milk**
**6 Tbsp (3½ fl oz/100 mL) vegetable oil**
**1½ cups (6 oz/175 g) flour**
**1¼ cups (3½ oz/100 g) grated cheese, such as mild cheddar**
**1 Tbsp baking powder**
**salt, pepper**

Preheat the oven to 350°F (180°C).

Combine the eggs, milk, and oil in a large mixing bowl and beat together. Add the flour and grated cheese. Season with salt and pepper, and stir to combine. Gently fold in the baking powder.

Transfer to the pan and bake for about 50 minutes. Let cool in the pan before turning out.

### CLASSIC COMBINATIONS

Before you begin to experiment, here are some suggestions for tried-and-tested combinations that are sure to please everyone. Starting with these will guarantee success and inspire you to branch out on your own.

Spinach and nutmeg

Chicken and curry

Salmon and dill

Mustard and tarragon

Mushrooms and parsley

### SOMETHING DIFFERENT

As your cake-baking skills grow, you will want to experiment with more adventurous combinations. Be inspired by the particular taste sensations you enjoy to come up with some original cake recipes. Consider also exciting color combinations like green and black, orange and green, green and yellow, yellow and black.

When you travel, it is always an idea to make a note of unusual ingredients and taste combinations that you have discovered and enjoyed. Back home, it's fun to try to recreate these exotic partnerships.

### MILK

When making sweet cakes that contain whole-wheat flour, I often use buttermilk. This ingredient lends a pleasant acidic tang and blends well with butter and oil since it is a natural emulsifier. It is also easier to digest than ordinary milk. Alternatively, you can use regular milk acidulated with a few drops of lemon juice or vinegar. You can also use yogurt or crème fraîche.

### OIL

Any single-plant vegetable oil can be used, such as sunflower, rapeseed or peanut, but mixed vegetable oils are also suitable. These are neutral in taste and clear in color.

If you want to go for something a little more out of the ordinary, try using walnut, olive, or hazelnut oil. These oils will add a touch of originality and subtle surprise to your creations.

### HERBS

It is always preferable to use fresh herbs rather than dried or frozen as these have the best flavor. They also add more color to the finished cake.

### SPICES

Don't be afraid to experiment with lots of different spices, alone or in combinations of your own choosing. All of the following will lend something unique and special to your cakes: nutmeg, turmeric, ginger, paprika, chili, cumin, coriander seed, cinnamon, and all sorts of peppercorns.

Buy your spices in small quantities and store in sealed containers for maximum freshness. If you have a mortar and pestle, or a spice grinder, choose whole spices to grind yourself.

The savory cake kit

flour

eggs

oil

cheese for grating

milk

salt + pepper

herbs

# A FEW SIDE SALADS

HERE ARE SOME IDEAS TO SERVE WITH YOUR SAVORY CAKES. EACH SALAD WILL SERVE 4-6 PEOPLE BUT YOU CAN EASILY INCREASE OR DECREASE THE QUANTITIES TO SUIT. DO NOT PREPARE YOUR SALADS UNTIL YOU ARE READY TO EAT, AS ONCE THEY ARE DRESSED WITH OIL AND VINEGAR THE LEAVES WILT QUICKLY.

## CHERRY TOMATO, SHALLOT, AND CILANTRO

Preparation time: 10 minutes

1¼ lb (600 g) cherry tomatoes
1 shallot
1 small bunch of cilantro
olive oil
balsamic vinegar
salt, pepper

Halve the cherry tomatoes. Peel the shallot and chop finely. Wash the cilantro and chop coarsely. Combine the tomatoes, shallot, and cilantro in a bowl. Add the oil and vinegar and mix well. Season with salt and pepper.

Variation  Replace the shallot with scallions, add a handful of freshly shelled peas and use parsley in place of the cilantro.

## GREEN BEANS, FETA, AND SUN-DRIED TOMATOES

Preparation time: 20 minutes

1¼ lb (600 g) green beans, fresh or frozen
7 oz (200 g) feta cheese
5 sun-dried tomatoes
1 tsp capers
olive oil
juice of ½ lemon
salt, pepper

Trim the green beans and cook in boiling water for 6 minutes; they should still be crunchy. Cut the feta into cubes. Combine the sun-dried tomatoes and some oil in a food processor and mix to a purée. Add the capers and process a few more times. Combine the green beans with the caper mixture and mix well. Stir in some more oil and the lemon juice. Season with salt and pepper.

Variation  Use marinated artichokes in place of the sun-dried tomatoes.

## ZUCCHINI AND BLACK SESAME SEED

Preparation time: 15 minutes

4-5 small, firm zucchini
2 tsp black sesame seeds
olive oil
juice of 1 lemon
pinch of sugar
salt, pepper

Julienne the zucchini using a mandolin slicer. Dry-fry the sesame seeds in a frying pan. Combine the zucchini and sesame seeds in a bowl. Add the oil and lemon juice and mix well. Add the sugar, season with salt and pepper.

## BEET, MOZZARELLA, AND LIME

Preparation time: 15 minutes

2-3 cooked beets
7 oz (200 g) mozzarella cheese
1-2 red Belgian endive
juice of 2 limes
grated zest of 1 lime
olive oil
pinch of sugar
salt, pepper

Cut the beets. Separate the Belgian endives and chop coarsely. Use your fingers to tear apart the mozzarella cheese. Combine these ingredients and mix well. Dissolve the sugar in the lime juice. Add the lime juice and zest to the beet mixture and mix well. Drizzle with oil and season with salt and pepper.

Variation  Replace the Belgian endive with radishes and season with dry-roasted sesame seeds. You can also add a handful of chopped fresh herbs such as basil or dill.

ADD GRATED VEGETABLES TO YOUR CAKE
BATTER FOR A DELICATE MELTING TEXTURE.

## ZUCCHINI AND PARMESAN CAKE

Preparation time: 15 minutes
Cooking time: 50 minutes

**2 zucchini**
**handful of fresh mint leaves**
**handful of fresh basil**
**3 eggs**
**6 Tbsp (3½ fl oz/100 mL) low-fat milk**
**6 Tbsp (3½ fl oz/100 mL) olive oil**
**1½ cups (6 oz/175 g) flour**
**1¼ cups (3½ oz/100 g) grated cheese, such as mild cheddar**
**1 cup (3½ oz/100 g) grated Parmesan**
**1 Tbsp baking powder**
**salt, pepper**

Preheat the oven to 350°F (180°C). Butter and flour
a cake pan.

Wash the zucchini, then grate finely. Chop the mint
and basil finely.

Combine the eggs, milk, and oil in a large mixing
bowl and beat together. Add the flour, grated
cheeses, herbs, and zucchini. Season with salt and
pepper, and stir to combine. Gently fold in the
baking powder.

Transfer to the prepared pan and bake for about
50 minutes. Let cool in the pan before turning out.

## PUMPKIN AND CHILI CAKE

Preparation time: 15 minutes
Cooking time: 50 minutes

**7 oz (200 g) peeled pumpkin**
**3 eggs**
**6 Tbsp (3½ fl oz/100 mL) low-fat milk**
**6 Tbsp (3½ fl oz/100 mL) olive oil**
**1½ cups (6 oz/175 g) flour**
**1¼ cups (3½ oz/100 g) grated cheese, such as mild cheddar**
**1 cup (3½ oz/100 g) grated Parmesan**
**1 tsp finely ground chilis**
**handful of pine nuts**
**1 Tbsp baking powder**
**salt, pepper**

Preheat the oven to 350°F (180°C). Butter and flour
a cake pan.

Grate the pumpkin coarsely. Using your hands,
squeeze out any excess moisture.

Combine the eggs, milk, oil, Parmesan, and pumpkin
in a large mixing bowl and beat together. Add the
flour, grated cheese, chili, and pine nuts. Season
with salt and pepper, and stir to combine. Gently
fold in the baking powder.

Transfer to the prepared pan and bake for about
50 minutes. Let cool in the pan before turning out.

## PARSNIP AND THYME CAKE

Preparation time: 15 minutes
Cooking time: 50 minutes

**1 large parsnip**
**bunch of fresh thyme**
**3 eggs**
**6 Tbsp (3½ fl oz/100 mL) low-fat milk**
**6 Tbsp (3½ fl oz/100 mL) walnut or hazelnut oil**
**1½ cups (6 oz/175 g) flour**
**1¼ cups (3½ oz/100 g) grated cheese, such as mild cheddar**
**1 Tbsp baking powder**
**salt, pepper**

Preheat the oven to 350°F (180°C). Butter and flour
a cake pan.

Peel the parsnip and grate coarsely. Strip the
thyme leaves from the stems.

Combine the eggs, milk, and oil in a large mixing
bowl and beat together. Add the flour, grated
cheeses, parsnip, and thyme leaves. Season with
salt and pepper, and stir to combine. Gently fold in
the baking powder.

Transfer to the prepared pan and bake for about
50 minutes. Let cool in the pan before turning out.

## BACON AND CARROT CAKE

Preparation time: 15 minutes
Cooking time: 50 minutes

2 carrots
handful of fresh tarragon
3 eggs
6 Tbsp (3½ fl oz/100 mL) low-fat milk
6 Tbsp (3½ fl oz/100 mL) vegetable oil
1½ cups (6 oz/175 g) flour
1¼ cups (3½ oz/100 g) grated cheese, such as mild cheddar
3½ oz (100 g) bacon, cut in cubes or coarsely chopped
1 Tbsp baking powder
salt, pepper

Preheat the oven to 350°F (180°C). Butter and flour a cake pan.

Peel the carrots and grate coarsely. Finely chop the tarragon.

Combine the eggs, milk, and oil in a large mixing bowl and beat together. Add the flour, grated cheese, carrots, bacon, and tarragon. Season with salt and pepper, and stir to combine. Gently fold in the baking powder.

Transfer to the prepared pan and bake for about 50 minutes. Let cool in the pan before turning out.

## CHESTNUT AND CELERY CAKE

Preparation time: 15 minutes
Cooking time: 50 minutes

2 celery stalks
5 oz (150 g) chestnuts, canned or frozen
3 eggs
6 Tbsp (3½ fl oz/100 mL) low-fat milk
6 Tbsp (3½ fl oz/100 mL) walnut oil
1½ cups (6 oz/175 g) flour
1¼ cups (3½ oz/100 g) grated cheese, such as mild cheddar
1 Tbsp baking powder
salt, pepper

Preheat the oven to 350°F (180°C). Butter and flour a cake pan.

Trim the celery ends and chop finely; do not use the leafy ends as they can be bitter. Chop the chestnuts coarsely.

Combine the eggs, milk, and oil in a large mixing bowl and beat together. Add the flour, grated cheese, celery, and chestnuts. Season with salt and pepper, and stir to combine. Gently fold in the baking powder.

Transfer to the prepared pan and bake for about 50 minutes. Let cool in the pan before turning out.

## CARROT AND ZUCCHINI CAKE

Preparation time: 15 minutes
Cooking time: 50 minutes

1 carrot
1 zucchini
handful of fresh mint leaves
3 eggs
6 Tbsp (3½ fl oz/100 mL) low-fat milk
6 Tbsp (3½ fl oz/100 mL) olive oil
1½ cups (6 oz/175 g) flour
1¼ cups (3½ oz/100 g) grated cheese, such as mild cheddar
1 Tbsp baking powder
salt, pepper

Preheat the oven to 350°F (180°C). Butter and flour a cake pan.

Peel the carrot. Grate the carrot, and zucchini coarsely. Finely chop the mint.

Combine the eggs, milk, oil, carrot, and zucchini in a large mixing bowl and beat together. Add the flour, grated cheese, and the mint. Season with salt and pepper, and stir to combine. Gently fold in the baking powder.

Transfer to the prepared pan and bake for about 50 minutes. Let cool in the pan before turning out.

## BELL PEPPER AND CUMIN CAKE

Preparation time: 15 minutes
Cooking time: 50 minutes

1 bell pepper, red or yellow
3 eggs
6 Tbsp (3½ fl oz/100 mL) low-fat milk
6 Tbsp (3½ fl oz/100 mL) olive oil
1½ cups (6 oz/175 g) flour
1¼ cups (3½ oz/100 g) grated cheese, such as mild cheddar
1 tsp ground cumin
1 Tbsp baking powder
salt, pepper

Preheat the oven to 350°F (180°C). Butter and flour a cake pan.

Wash the pepper and chop finely.

Combine the eggs, milk, and oil in a large mixing bowl and beat together. Add the flour, grated cheese, pepper, and cumin. Season with salt and pepper, and stir to combine. Gently fold in the baking powder.

Transfer to the prepared pan and bake for about 50 minutes. Let cool in the pan before turning out.

# ROASTED VEGETABLE CAKE

Preparation time: 30 minutes
Cooking time: 50 minutes

**1 carrot**
**1 zucchini**
**1 leek**
**1 bell pepper, any color**
**handful of fresh thyme**
**3 eggs**
**6 Tbsp (3½ fl oz/100 mL) low-fat milk**
**6 Tbsp (3½ fl oz/100 mL) olive oil, plus extra for roasting**
**the vegetables**
**1½ cups (6 oz/175 g) flour**
**1¼ cups (3½ oz/100 g) grated cheese, such as mild cheddar**
**1 Tbsp baking powder**
**salt, pepper**

Preheat the oven to 350°F (180°C). Butter and flour a cake pan.

Peel the carrot. Wash the zucchini and leek. Slice all the vegetables into thin sticks. Strip the thyme leaves from the stalks.

Put the vegetables in a baking dish lined with baking paper to prevent them from sticking. Drizzle with oil and add the thyme. Season with salt and pepper. Use your hands to mix well. Roast for 20–30 minutes.

Combine the eggs, milk, and oil in a large mixing bowl and beat together. Add the roasted vegetables reserving a few for garnish. Add the flour and grated cheese. Season with salt and pepper, and stir to combine. Gently fold in the baking powder.

Transfer to the prepared pan, arrange the reserved vegetables on top and bake for about 50 minutes. Let cool in the pan before turning out.

Tip  You can increase the amount of vegetables you roast as they make a delicious accompaniment to the finished cake.

## PARSLEY AND CHILI CAKE

Preparation time: 10 minutes
Cooking time: 50 minutes

2 large handfuls of fresh parsley
2 cloves garlic
2 red chilis
handful of pine nuts (optional)
3 eggs
6 Tbsp (3½ fl oz/100 mL) low-fat milk
6 Tbsp (3½ fl oz/100 mL) olive oil
1½ cups (6 oz/175 g) flour
1¼ cups (3½ oz/100 g) grated cheese, such as mild cheddar
1 cup (3½ oz/100 g) grated Parmesan
1 Tbsp baking powder
salt, pepper

Preheat the oven to 350°F (180°C). Butter and flour a cake pan.

Chop the parsley coarsely. Peel the garlic and crush. Halve the chilis lengthwise. With the tip of a small knife, remove the seeds then slice thinly.

Combine the eggs, milk, and oil in a large mixing bowl and beat together. Add the flour and grated cheeses, parsley, garlic, chilis, and pine nuts if using. Season with salt and pepper, and stir to combine. Gently fold in the baking powder.

Transfer to the prepared pan and bake for about 50 minutes. Let cool in the pan before turning out.

## WATERCRESS AND SWEET POTATO CAKE

Preparation time: 15 minutes
Cooking time: 50 minutes

bunch of watercress
1 sweet potato
3 eggs
½ cup (4 fl oz/125 mL) low-fat milk
6 Tbsp (3½ fl oz/100 mL) vegetable oil
1½ cups (6 oz/175 g) flour
1¼ cups (3½ oz/100 g) grated cheese, such as mild cheddar
1 Tbsp baking powder
salt, pepper

Preheat the oven to 350°F (180°C). Butter and flour a cake pan.

Wash the watercress and coarsely chop the leaves. Peel the sweet potato and grate coarsely.

Combine the eggs, milk, oil, watercress, and sweet potato in a large mixing bowl and beat together. Add the flour and grated cheese. Season with salt and pepper, and stir to combine. Gently fold in the baking powder.

Transfer to the prepared pan and bake for about 50 minutes. Let cool in the pan before turning out.

Tip  You can also add a pinch of ground cumin to the mixture.

## MUSHROOM AND PARSLEY CAKE

Preparation time: 15 minutes
Cooking time: 50 minutes

10 oz (300 g) mixed mushrooms
2 shallots
handful of flat-leaf parsley
knob of butter
3 eggs
6 Tbsp (3½ fl oz/100 mL) low-fat milk
6 Tbsp (3½ fl oz/100 mL) walnut oil
1½ cups (6 oz/175 g) flour
1¼ cups (3½ oz/100 g) grated cheese, such as mild cheddar
1 Tbsp baking powder
salt, pepper

Preheat the oven to 350°F (180°C). Butter and flour a cake pan.

Clean the mushrooms and slice. Peel the shallots and chop finely. Chop the parsley.

Melt the butter in a small pan over high heat. Add the mushrooms and cook until all the liquid evaporates. Stir in the shallots and parsley and cook for a further 2 minutes. Set aside to cool.

Combine the eggs, milk, and oil in a large mixing bowl and beat together. Add the flour, grated cheese, and mushroom mixture. Season with salt and pepper, and stir to combine. Gently fold in the baking powder.

Transfer to the prepared pan and bake for about 50 minutes. Let cool in the pan before turning out.

## SHRIMP AND SORREL CAKE

Preparation time: 15 minutes
Cooking time: 50 minutes

5 oz (150 g) peeled and deveined shrimp
bunch of sorrel
3 eggs
6 Tbsp (3½ fl oz/100 mL) low-fat milk
6 Tbsp (3½ fl oz/100 mL) vegetable oil
1½ cups (6 oz/175 g) flour
1¼ cups (3½ oz/100 g) grated cheese, such as mild cheddar
1 Tbsp baking powder
salt, pepper

Preheat the oven to 350°F (180°C). Butter and flour a cake pan.

Chop the shrimp. Chop the sorrel coarsely.

Combine the eggs, milk, and oil in a large mixing bowl and beat together. Add the flour, grated cheese, shrimp, and sorrel. Season with salt and pepper, and stir to combine. Gently fold in the baking powder.

Transfer to the prepared pan and bake for about 50 minutes. Let cool in the pan before turning out.

## GREEN AND BLACK CAKE

Preparation time: 15 minutes
Cooking time: 50 minutes

**2 Tbsp black sesame seeds**
**handful of cilantro leaves**
**3 eggs**
**6 Tbsp (3½ fl oz/100 mL) low-fat milk**
**6 Tbsp (3½ fl oz/100 mL) hazelnut oil**
**1½ cups (6 oz/175 g) flour**
**1¼ cups (3½ oz/100 g) grated cheese, such as mild cheddar**
**1 cup (3½ oz/100 g) grated Parmesan**
**1½ cups (5 oz/150 g) petits pois, fresh or frozen**
**1 Tbsp baking powder**
**salt, pepper**

Preheat the oven to 350°F (180°C). Butter and flour a cake pan.

In a small pan, dry-fry the sesame seeds to enhance their taste. Chop the cilantro coarsely.

Combine the eggs, milk, and oil in a large mixing bowl and beat together. Add the flour, grated cheeses, sesame seeds, cilantro, and peas. Season with salt and pepper, and stir to combine. Gently fold in the baking powder.

Transfer to the prepared pan and bake for about 50 minutes. Let cool in the pan before turning out.

Note  If using fresh peas, allow about 10 oz (300 g) unshelled peas to yield the required amount. Frozen peas do not need to be defrosted.

## TWO-OLIVE CAKE

Preparation time: 10 minutes
Cooking time: 50 minutes

3 eggs
6 Tbsp (3½ fl oz/100 mL) low-fat milk
6 Tbsp (3½ fl oz/100 mL) olive oil
1½ cups (6 oz/175 g) flour
1¼ cups (3½ oz/100 g) grated cheese, such as mild cheddar
3½ oz (100 g) smoked bacon, cut into pieces or cubes
3½ oz (100 g) pitted green olives, drained
3½ oz (100 g) pitted black olives
1 Tbsp baking powder
salt, pepper

Preheat the oven to 350°F (180°C). Butter and flour a cake pan.

Combine the eggs, milk, and oil in a large mixing bowl and beat together. Add the flour, grated cheese, bacon, and olives. Season with salt and pepper, and stir to combine. Gently fold in the baking powder.

Transfer to the prepared pan and bake for about 50 minutes. Let cool in the pan before turning out.

## EGGPLANT AND MINT CAKE

Preparation time: 15 minutes
Cooking time: 50 minutes

2 eggplants
handful of fresh mint leaves
3 eggs
6 Tbsp (3½ fl oz/100 mL) low-fat milk
6 Tbsp (3½ fl oz/100 mL) vegetable oil
1½ cups (6 oz/175 g) flour
1¼ cups (3½ oz/100 g) grated cheese, such as mild cheddar
2 tsp tomato paste (optional)
1 Tbsp baking powder
salt, pepper

Preheat the oven to 350°F (180°C). Butter and flour a cake pan.

Pierce the eggplant all over with a fork. Cook in the microwave on medium for about 5 minutes, or until just tender. Cut in half, scoop out the flesh and chop finely. Finely chop the mint.

Combine the eggs, milk, and oil in a large mixing bowl and beat together. Add the flour, grated cheese, eggplant, mint, and tomato paste if using. Season with salt and pepper, and stir to combine. Gently fold in the baking powder.

Transfer to the prepared pan and bake for about 50 minutes. Let cool in the pan before turning out.

## SPINACH AND GARBANZO BEAN CAKE

Preparation time: 15 minutes
Cooking time: 50 minutes

3½ oz (100 g) fresh spinach
3 eggs
6 Tbsp (3½ fl oz/100 mL) low-fat milk
6 Tbsp (3½ fl oz/100 mL) vegetable oil
1½ cups (6 oz/175 g) flour
1¼ cups (3½ oz/100 g) grated cheese, such as mild cheddar
3½ oz (100 g) canned garbanzo beans, drained
1 tsp curry powder
1 Tbsp baking powder
salt, pepper

Preheat the oven to 350°F (180°C). Butter and flour a cake pan.

Wash and dry the spinach, then chop coarsely.

Combine the eggs, milk, and oil in a large mixing bowl and beat together. Add the flour, grated cheese, spinach, garbanzo beans, and curry powder. Season with salt and pepper, and stir to combine. Gently fold in the baking powder.

Transfer to the prepared pan and bake for about 50 minutes. Let cool in the pan before turning out.

Note  In this recipe the spinach is used like fresh herbs so do not substitute frozen.

PARMESAN, GOUDA, GOAT, BLUE… COMBINE
YOUR FAVORITE CHEESES WITH HERBS, SPICES,
OR DRY FRUIT.

## ROQUEFORT CAKE

Preparation time: 15 minutes
Cooking time: 50 minutes

5 oz (150 g) Roquefort cheese
1 pear
6 Tbsp (about 2 oz/60 g) walnuts
3 eggs
6 Tbsp (3½ fl oz/100 mL) low-fat milk
3 Tbsp (1½ fl oz/45 mL) walnut oil
3 Tbsp (1½ fl oz/45 mL) olive oil
1½ cups (6 oz/175 g) flour
1¼ cups (3½ oz/100 g) grated cheese, such as mild cheddar
1 Tbsp baking powder
salt, pepper

Preheat the oven to 350°F (180°C). Butter and flour
a cake pan.

Crumble the Roquefort into pieces. Cut the pear
into small pieces. Coarsely chop the walnuts.

Combine the eggs, milk, and oil in a large mixing
bowl and beat together. Add the flour, grated
cheese, Roquefort, pear, and walnut pieces. Season
with salt and pepper, and stir to combine. Gently
fold in the baking powder.

Transfer to the prepared pan and bake for about
50 minutes. Let cool in the pan before turning out.

## GOAT CHEESE CAKE

Preparation time: 10 minutes
Cooking time: 50 minutes

1 small firm goat cheese, about 2 oz (60 g)
handful of fresh rosemary leaves
3 eggs
6 Tbsp (3½ fl oz/100 mL) low-fat milk
6 Tbsp (3½ fl oz/100 mL) olive oil
1¼ cups (7 oz/200 g) flour
10–15 raisins
1 Tbsp baking powder
salt, pepper

Preheat the oven to 350°F (180°C). Butter and flour
a cake pan.

Cut the goat cheese into pieces. Strip the
rosemary leaves from the stems and chop finely.

Combine the eggs, milk, and oil in a large mixing
bowl and beat together. Add the flour, goat
cheese, raisins, and rosemary. Season with salt
and pepper, and stir to combine. Gently fold in the
baking powder.

Transfer to the prepared pan and bake for about
50 minutes. Let cool in the pan before turning out.

Note  This recipe is more successful made in individual
molds. In a large pan, the raisins tend to sink to the
bottom.

## PARMESAN CHEESE CAKE

Preparation time: 10 minutes
Cooking time: 50 minutes

2 oz (60 g) Parmesan cheese
3 tsp coriander seed
1 tsp Sichuan peppercorns
1 tsp black peppercorns
2 juniper berries (optional)
3 eggs
6 Tbsp (3½ fl oz/100 mL) low-fat milk
6 Tbsp (3½ fl oz/100 mL) vegetable oil
1½ cups (6 oz/175 g) flour
1¼ cups (3½ oz/100 g) grated cheese, such as mild cheddar
1 cup (3½ oz/100 g) grated Parmesan
1 Tbsp baking powder
salt

Preheat the oven to 350°F (180°C). Butter and flour
a cake pan.

Using a sharp knife, chop the Parmesan into coarse
crumbs. Grind the spices to a powder in a mortar
and pestle.

Combine the eggs, milk, and oil in a large mixing
bowl and beat together. Add the flour, grated
cheese, grated Parmesan, and ground spices.
Season with salt and mix to combine. Gently fold in
the baking powder.

Transfer to the prepared pan and bake for about
50 minutes. Let cool in the pan before turning out.

## QUARK CHEESE CAKE

Preparation time: 15 minutes
Cooking time: 50 minutes

**large handful of fresh chives**
**3 eggs**
**6 Tbsp (3½ fl oz/100 mL) vegetable oil**
**7 oz (200 g) fromage frais or quark**
**1¼ cups (7 oz/200 g) flour**
**2 tsp ground chilis or hot paprika**
**1 Tbsp baking powder**
**salt, pepper**

Preheat the oven to 350°F (180°C). Butter and flour a cake pan.

Finely chop the chives.

Combine the eggs, oil, and quark in a large mixing bowl and beat together. Add the flour, chives, and chili. Season with salt and pepper, and stir to combine. Gently fold in the baking powder.

Transfer to the prepared pan and bake for about 50 minutes. Let cool in the pan before turning out.

## MIMOLETTE CHEESE CAKE

Preparation: 10 minutes
Cooking time: 50 minutes

**3 eggs**
**6 Tbsp (3½ fl oz/100 mL) low-fat milk**
**6 Tbsp (3½ fl oz/100 mL) vegetable oil**
**1½ cups (6 oz/175 g) flour**
**1¼ cups (3½ oz/100 g) grated Mimolette cheese (or Gouda)**
**1¼ cups (3½ oz/100 g) diced Mimolette cheese (or Gouda)**
**2 tsp whole caraway seed**
**1 Tbsp baking powder**
**salt, pepper**

Preheat the oven to 350°F (180°C). Butter and flour a cake pan.

Combine the eggs, milk, and oil in a large mixing bowl and beat together. Add the flour, the grated and the diced Mimolette, and caraway seed. Season with salt and pepper, and stir to combine. Gently fold in the baking powder.

Transfer to the prepared pan and bake for about 50 minutes. Let cool in the pan before turning out.

Note  Caraway seed tastes similar to cumin but is less intense. In India, this spice is used to enhance curries, lentil and rice dishes. In Eastern European countries, it is used with cured meats, sauerkraut, and fish dishes. This spice is widely available in large supermarkets.

## FETA CHEESE AND HERB CAKE

Preparation time: 15 minutes
Cooking time: 50 minutes

**7 oz (200 g) feta cheese**
**2–3 handfuls of mixed fresh herbs (basil, mint, parsley, and chives)**
**3 eggs**
**6 Tbsp (3½ fl oz/100 mL) low-fat milk**
**6 Tbsp (3½ fl oz/100 mL) olive oil**
**1½ cups (6 oz/175 g) flour**
**1¼ cups (3½ oz/100 g) grated cheese, such as mild cheddar**
**1 Tbsp baking powder**
**salt, pepper**

Preheat the oven to 350°F (180°C). Butter and flour a cake pan.

Cut the feta into cubes. Coarsely chop the herbs.

Combine the eggs, milk, and oil in a large mixing bowl and beat together. Add the flour, grated cheese, feta, and herbs. Season with salt and pepper, and stir to combine. Gently fold in the baking powder.

Transfer to the prepared pan and bake for about 50 minutes. Let cool in the pan before turning out.

WITH SO MANY DELICIOUS INGREDIENTS TO
CHOOSE FROM—HAM, SAUSAGE, BACON, FOIE
GRAS, AND DUCK CONFIT—FEW WILL BE ABLE
TO KEEP AWAY FROM THESE CAKES.

## HAM AND SAGE CAKE

Preparation time: 10 minutes
Cooking time: 50 minutes

3½ oz (100 g) fatback pork or pork belly
several fresh sage leaves
3 eggs
6 Tbsp (3½ fl oz/100 mL) low-fat milk
6 Tbsp (3½ fl oz/100 mL) vegetable oil
1½ cups + 2 Tbsp (3½ oz/100 g) flour
½ cup (2½ oz/80 g) whole-wheat flour
1¼ cups (3½ oz/100 g) grated cheese, such as mild cheddar
1 Tbsp baking powder
salt, pepper

Preheat the oven to 350°F (180°C). Butter and flour
a cake pan.

Cut the pork into small pieces. Finely chop the
sage leaves.

Combine the eggs, milk, and oil in a large mixing
bowl and beat together. Add the flours, grated
cheese, pork, and sage. Season with salt and
pepper, and stir to combine. Gently fold in the
baking powder.

Transfer to the prepared pan and bake for about
50 minutes. Let cool in the pan before turning out.

## FIG AND CURED HAM CAKE

Preparation time: 15 minutes
Cooking time: 50 minutes

7 oz (200 g) ripe figs
3½ oz (100 g) cured ham slices
3 eggs
6 Tbsp (3½ fl oz/100 mL) low-fat milk
6 Tbsp (3½ fl oz/100 mL) vegetable oil
1½ cups (6 oz/175 g) flour
1¼ cups (3½ oz/100 g) grated cheese, such as mild cheddar
1 Tbsp baking powder
salt, pepper

Preheat the oven to 350°F (180°C). Butter and flour
a cake pan.

Cut the figs into pieces. Using your hands, tear the
ham into small pieces.

Combine the eggs, milk, and oil in a large mixing
bowl and beat together. Add the flour, grated
cheese, figs, and ham. Season with salt and
pepper, and stir to combine. Gently fold in the
baking powder.

Transfer to the prepared pan and bake for about
50 minutes. Let cool in the pan before turning out.

## DELI CAKE

Preparation time: 10 minutes
Cooking time: 50 minutes

2 oz (60 g) bacon
3½ oz (100 g) saucisson sec (see note)
3½ oz (100 g) chorizo sausage
handful of hazelnuts
3 eggs
6 Tbsp (3½ fl oz/100 mL) low-fat milk
6 Tbsp (3½ fl oz/100 mL) walnut oil
1½ cups (6 oz/175 g) flour
1¼ cups (3½ oz/100 g) grated cheese, such as mild cheddar
1 Tbsp baking powder
salt, pepper

Preheat the oven to 350°F (180°C). Butter and flour
a cake pan.

Cut the bacon, saucisson sec, and chorizo into
small pieces. Use a mortar and pestle, or a knife,
to coarsely chop the hazelnuts.

Combine the eggs, milk, and oil in a large mixing
bowl and beat together. Add the flour, cheese,
bacon, saucisson sec, chorizo, and hazelnuts.
Season with salt and pepper, and stir to combine.
Gently fold in the baking powder.

Transfer to the prepared pan and bake for about
50 minutes. Let cool in the pan before turning out.

Note  Saucisson sec is French-style dry-cured salami.

## SMOKED CHICKEN DILL CAKE

Preparation time: 15 minutes
Cooking time: 50 minutes

**7 oz (200 g) smoked chicken**
**2 handfuls of fresh dill**
**3 eggs**
**6 Tbsp (3½ fl oz/100 mL) low-fat milk**
**6 Tbsp (3½ fl oz/100 mL) vegetable oil**
**1½ cups (6 oz/175 g) flour**
**1¼ cups (3½ oz/100 g) grated cheese, such as mild cheddar**
**1 Tbsp baking powder**
**salt, pepper**

Preheat the oven to 350°F (180°C). Butter and flour a cake pan.

Cut the chicken into small pieces. Coarsely chop the dill.

Combine the eggs, milk, and oil in a large mixing bowl and beat together. Add the flour, grated cheese, chicken, and dill. Season with salt and pepper, and mix to obtain a smooth batter. Gently fold in the baking powder.

Transfer to the prepared pan and bake for about 50 minutes. Let cool in the pan before turning out.

# DUCK CONFIT CAKE

Preparation time: 15 minutes
Cooking time: 50 minutes

**1 duck confit, thigh piece**
**2 plums**
**3 eggs**
**6 Tbsp (3½ fl oz/100 mL) low-fat milk**
**6 Tbsp (3½ fl oz/100 mL) vegetable oil**
**¼ tsp ground cinnamon**
**1½ cups (6 oz/175 g) flour**
**1¼ cups (3½ oz/100 g) grated cheese, such as mild cheddar**
**1 Tbsp baking powder**
**salt, pepper**

Preheat the oven to 350°F (180°C). Butter and flour
a cake pan.

Cut the skin away from the duck meat. Shred the
meat into large pieces. Cut the prunes into pieces.

Combine the eggs, milk, and oil in a large mixing
bowl and beat together. Add the flour, cheese,
duck, prunes, and cinnamon. Season with salt and
pepper, and stir to combine. Gently fold in the
baking powder.

Transfer to the prepared pan and bake for about
50 minutes. Let cool in the pan before turning out.

USING INSPIRATION FROM YOUR TRAVELS IS A
GREAT WAY TO CREATE RECIPES. PERHAPS ONE
OF THESE RECIPES WILL REMIND YOU OF
HOLIDAYS PAST.

## ITALIAN CAKE

Preparation time: 15 minutes
Cooking time: 50 minutes

**large handful of arugula**
**5oz (150 g) pancetta or bacon (see note)**
**3 eggs**
**6 Tbsp (3½ fl oz/100 mL) low-fat milk**
**6 Tbsp (3½ fl oz/100 mL) vegetable oil**
**1½ cups (6 oz/175 g) flour**
**1¼ cups (3½ oz/100 g) grated cheese, such as mild cheddar**
**1 cup (3½ oz/100 g) grated Parmesan cheese**
**1 Tbsp baking powder**
**salt, pepper**

Preheat the oven to 350°F (180°C). Butter and flour
a cake pan.

Coarsely chop the arugula. Cut the pancetta into
small pieces.

Combine the eggs, milk, and oil in a large mixing
bowl and beat together. Add the flour, cheeses,
arugula, and pancetta. Season with salt and
pepper, and stir to combine. Gently fold in the
baking powder.

Transfer to the prepared pan and bake for about
50 minutes. Let cool in the pan before turning out.

Note  Pancetta is Italian-style bacon and can be found in
specialty stores.

## SCANDINAVIAN CAKE

Preparation time: 15 minutes
Cooking time: 50 minutes

3½ oz (100 g) smoked salmon
handful of fresh dill
2 Tbsp red peppercorns
3 eggs
6 Tbsp (3½ fl oz/100 mL) low-fat milk
6 Tbsp (3½ fl oz/100 mL) vegetable oil
1½ cups (6 oz/175 g) flour
1¼ cups (3½ oz/100 g) grated cheese, such as mild cheddar
1 Tbsp baking powder
salt, pepper

Preheat the oven to 350°F (180°C). Butter and flour a cake pan.

Cut the salmon into thin strips. Coarsely chop the dill. Using a mortar and pestle, grind the peppercorns.

Combine the eggs, milk, and oil in a large mixing bowl and beat together. Add the flour, cheese, salmon, dill, and peppercorns. Season with salt and pepper, and stir to combine. Gently fold in the baking powder.

Transfer to the prepared pan and bake for about 50 minutes. Let cool in the pan before turning out.

Tip  Make individual cakes using a muffin pan. To serve, cut the cakes in half and fill each with a spoonful of ricotta cheese that has been mixed with a few teaspoons of grated horseradish.

## BEER CAKE

Preparation time: 10 minutes
Cooking time: 50 minutes

6 Tbsp (3½ fl oz/100 mL) beer
3 eggs
6 Tbsp (3½ fl oz/100 mL) vegetable oil
1½ cups (6 oz/175 g) flour
1¼ cups (3½ oz/100 g) grated cheese, such as mild cheddar
3½ oz (100 g) dry onions
1 Tbsp baking powder
salt, pepper

Preheat the oven to 350°F (180°C). Butter and flour a cake pan.

In a large mixing bowl, combine the beer, eggs, and oil and beat together. Add the flour, cheese, and onions. Season with salt and pepper, and stir to combine. Gently fold in the baking powder.

Transfer to the prepared pan and bake for about 50 minutes. Let cool in the pan before turning out.

## BRETON-STYLE CAKE

Preparation time: 15 minutes
Cooking time: 50 minutes

1 leek
3 eggs
6 Tbsp (3½ fl oz/100 mL) low-fat milk
6 Tbsp (3½ fl oz/100 mL) vegetable oil
1½ cups (6 oz/175 g) flour
¾ cup (3½ oz/100 g) buckwheat flour
1¼ cups (3½ oz/100 g) grated cheese, such as mild cheddar
3½ oz (100 g) smoked bacon, cut into cubes or finely chopped
1 Tbsp baking powder
salt, pepper

Preheat the oven to 350°F (180°C). Butter and flour a cake pan.

Rinse the leek and slice into thin rounds.

Combine the eggs, milk, and oil in a large mixing bowl and beat together. Add the flour, cheese, leeks, and bacon. Season with salt and pepper, and stir to combine. Gently fold in the baking powder.

Transfer to the prepared pan and bake for about 50 minutes. Let cool in the pan before turning out.

Tip  Serve this cake with glasses of chilled cider.

## THAI CAKE

Preparation time: 15 minutes
Cooking time: 50 minutes

**5 oz (150g) peeled and deveined shrimp**
**1 fresh red chili**
**3 eggs**
**6 Tbsp (3½ fl oz/100 mL) coconut milk**
**6 Tbsp (3½ fl oz/100 mL) vegetable oil**
**1½ cups (6 oz/175 g) flour**
**1¼ cups (3½ oz/100 g) grated cheese, such as mild cheddar**
**zest of 1 lime**
**juice of ½ lime**
**1 tsp turmeric**
**1 Tbsp baking powder**
**salt, pepper**

Preheat the oven to 350°F (180°C). Butter and flour a cake pan.

Chop the shrimp into pieces. Halve the chili. Using the tip of a small sharp knife, scrape out the seeds. Finely chop the chili.

Combine the eggs, coconut milk, and oil in a large mixing bowl and beat together. Add the flour, cheese, shrimp, chili, turmeric, and lime zest. Season with salt and pepper, and stir to combine. Gently fold in the baking powder.

Transfer to the prepared pan and bake for about 50 minutes. Let cool in the pan before turning out.

## SUSHI-STYLE CAKE

Preparation time: 10 minutes
Cooking time: 50 minutes

**3½ oz (100 g) smoked salmon**
**3 eggs**
**6 Tbsp (3½ fl oz/100 mL) crème fraîche or sour cream**
**6 Tbsp (3½ fl oz/100 mL) vegetable oil**
**1½ cups (6 oz/175 g) flour**
**4 tsp wasabi paste**
**1 Tbsp baking powder**
**salt, pepper**

Preheat the oven to 350°F (180°C). Butter and flour a cake pan.

Cut the salmon into thin strips.

Combine the eggs, oil, wasabi, and crème fraîche or sour cream in a large mixing bowl and beat together. Add the flour and salmon. Season with salt and pepper, and stir to combine. Gently fold in the baking powder.

Transfer to the prepared pan and bake for about 50 minutes. Let cool in the pan before turning out.

Note  You can use grated horseradish instead of wasabi paste.

## PROVENÇAL CAKE

Preparation time: 10 minutes
Cooking time: 50 minutes

**1 can (7 oz/200 g) tuna packed in water**
**handful of fresh thyme**
**3 eggs**
**6 Tbsp (3½ fl oz/100 mL) low-fat milk**
**6 Tbsp (3½ fl oz/100 mL) olive oil**
**1½ cups (6 oz/175 g) flour**
**1¼ cups (3½ oz/100 g) grated cheese, such as mild cheddar**
**zest of 1 lemon**
**1 Tbsp baking powder**
**salt, pepper**

Preheat the oven to 350°F (180°C). Butter and flour a cake pan.

Drain the tuna and flake with a fork. Coarsely chop the thyme.

Combine the eggs, milk, and oil in a large mixing bowl and beat together. Add the flour, cheese, tuna, thyme, and lemon zest. Season with salt and pepper, and stir to combine. Gently fold in the baking powder.

Transfer to the prepared pan and bake for about 50 minutes. Let cool in the pan before turning out.

Note  You can also add some black olives.

YOUR STORE CUPBOARD IS A GREAT SOURCE OF TASTY TREASURES: MUSTARD, CURRY PASTE, PESTO, CAPERS, HORSERADISH, AND CHUTNEYS. ANY NUMBER OF THESE WILL ADD ANOTHER DIMENSION TO YOUR SAVORY CAKES.

## PESTO AND PINE NUT CAKE

Preparation 10 minutes
Cooking time: 50 minutes

**large handful of pine nuts**
**3 eggs**
**6 Tbsp (3½ fl oz/100 mL) low-fat milk**
**3 Tbsp (1½ fl oz/50 mL) olive oil**
**1½ cups (6 oz/175 g) flour**
**1¼ cups (3½ oz/100 g) grated cheese, such as mild cheddar**
**3 Tbsp pesto**
**1 Tbsp baking powder**
**salt, pepper**

Preheat the oven to 350°F (180°C). Butter and flour a cake pan.

In a small frying pan, dry-fry the pine nuts until just brown to enhance their taste.

Combine the eggs, milk, and oil in a large mixing bowl and beat together. Add the flour, cheese, pine nuts, and pesto. Season with salt and pepper, and stir to combine. Gently fold in the baking powder.

Transfer to the prepared pan and bake for about 50 minutes. Let cool in the pan before turning out.

## PICCALILLI CAKE

Preparation time: 10 minutes
Cooking time: 50 minutes

**3 eggs**
**6 Tbsp (3½ fl oz/100 mL) low-fat milk**
**6 Tbsp (3½ fl oz/100 mL) vegetable oil**
**1½ cups (6 oz/175 g) flour**
**1¼ cups (3½ oz/100 g) grated cheese, such as mild cheddar**
**3 Tbsp Piccalilli or other mixed pickled vegetables**
**1 Tbsp baking powder**
**salt, pepper**

Preheat the oven to 350°F (180°C). Butter and flour a cake pan.

Combine the eggs, milk, and oil in a large mixing bowl and beat together. Add the flour, cheese, and Piccalilli. Season with salt and pepper, and stir to combine. Gently fold in the baking powder.

Transfer to the prepared pan and bake for about 50 minutes. Let cool in the pan before turning out.

## SUN-DRIED TOMATO CAKE

Preparation time: 15 minutes
Cooking time: 50 minutes

**7 oz (200 g) sun-dried tomatoes**
**3 Tbsp (2 oz/60 g) capers**
**3 eggs**
**6 Tbsp (3½ fl oz/100 mL) low-fat milk**
**6 Tbsp (3½ fl oz/100 mL) olive oil**
**1½ cups (6 oz/175 g) flour**
**1¼ cups (3½ oz/100 g) grated cheese, such as mild cheddar**
**2 Tbsp chopped fresh basil**
**1 Tbsp baking powder**
**salt, pepper**

Preheat the oven to 350°F (180°C). Butter and flour a cake pan.

Cut the sun-dried tomatoes into pieces.

Combine the eggs, milk, and oil in a large mixing bowl and beat together. Add the flour, cheese, sun-dried tomatoes, capers, and basil. Season with salt and pepper, and stir to combine. Gently fold in the baking powder.

Transfer to the prepared pan and bake for about 50 minutes. Let cool in the pan before turning out.

# SUN-DRIED TOMATO PASTE CAKE

Preparation 15 minutes
Cooking time: 50 minutes

**3 eggs**
**6 Tbsp (3½ fl oz/100 mL) low-fat milk**
**6 Tbsp (3½ fl oz/100 mL) olive oil**
**2 Tbsp sun-dried tomato paste**
**1½ cups (6 oz/200 g) flour**
**1¼ cups (3½ oz/100 g) grated cheese, such as mild cheddar**
**1 Tbsp baking powder**
**salt, pepper**

For the Sun-dried Tomato Paste
**5 oz (150 g) sun-dried tomatoes**
**large handful of pine nuts**
**4 Tbsp (2 fl oz/60 ml) olive oil (or use the oil from the
sun-dried tomatoes jar)**

Preheat the oven to 350°F (180°C). Butter and flour
a cake pan.

For the sun-dried tomato paste, combine all the
ingredients in the bowl of a food processor and mix
to obtain a smooth paste.

Combine the eggs, milk, oil, and tomato paste in a
large mixing bowl and beat together. Add the flour
and cheese. Season with salt and pepper, and stir
to combine. Gently fold in the baking powder.

Transfer to the prepared pan and bake for about
50 minutes. Let cool in the pan before turning out.

Note  Sun-dried tomato paste is a truly versatile
ingredient. You can also use it for canapés, by mixing
with some ricotta cheese and spreading on slices of
toasted bread. It also makes a delicious salad dressing.
Simply make a vinaigrette, replacing the mustard with
the tomato paste, and use balsamic vinegar and a good
olive oil.

## WILD MUSHROOM PESTO CAKE

Preparation time: 15 minutes
Cooking time: 50 minutes

bunch of fresh parsley
3 eggs
6 Tbsp (3½ fl oz/100 mL) low-fat milk
6 Tbsp (3½ fl oz/100 mL) olive oil
1½ cups (6 oz/175 g) flour
1¼ cups (3½ oz/100 g) grated cheese, such as mild cheddar
3 Tbsp wild mushroom pesto (see below)
1 Tbsp baking powder
salt, pepper

For the Wild Mushroom Pesto
5 oz (150 g) wild mushrooms, such as ceps (porcini)
3½ oz (100g) cultivated mushrooms
handful of pine nuts
1 clove garlic
4 Tbsp (2 fl oz/60 ml) olive oil
salt, pepper

Preheat the oven to 350°F (180°C). Butter and flour a cake pan.

For the pesto, combine all the ingredients in the bowl of a food processor and mix to obtain a smooth paste. Finely chop the parsley.

Combine the eggs, milk, oil, and pesto in a large mixing bowl and beat together. Add the flour, cheese, and parsley. Season with salt and pepper, and stir to combine. Gently fold in the baking powder.

Transfer to the prepared pan and bake for about 50 minutes. Let cool in the pan before turning out.

## CHICKEN AND CURRY CAKE

Preparation time: 15 minutes
Cooking time: 50 minutes

5 oz (150 g) roast chicken
3 eggs
6 Tbsp (3½ fl oz/100 mL) low-fat milk
6 Tbsp (3½ fl oz/100 mL) vegetable oil
2 tsp curry paste
1¼ cups (7 oz/200 g) flour
1¼ cups (3½ oz/100 g) grated cheese, such as mild cheddar
1 handful of chopped fresh tarragon (optional)
1 Tbsp baking powder
salt, pepper

Preheat the oven to 350°F (180°C). Butter and flour a cake pan.

Remove any bones from the chicken meat and chop it coarsely.

Combine the eggs, milk, oil, and curry paste in a large mixing bowl and beat together. Add the flour, cheese, chicken, and tarragon. Season with salt and pepper, and stir to combine. Gently fold in the baking powder.

Transfer to the prepared pan and bake for about 50 minutes. Let cool in the pan before turning out.

Note  You could also add some chopped cilantro or flat-leaf parsley.

## APPLE AND HORSERADISH CAKE

Preparation time: 10 minutes
Cooking time: 50 minutes

1 apple
3 eggs
6 Tbsp (3½ fl oz/100 mL) low-fat milk
6 Tbsp (3½ fl oz/100 mL) vegetable oil
5 tsp grated horseradish
1¾ cups (7 oz/200 g) flour
1¼ cups (3½ oz/100 g) grated cheese, such as mild cheddar
1 Tbsp baking powder
salt, pepper

Preheat the oven to 350°F (180°C). Butter and flour a cake pan.

Wash the apple and chop finely. There is no need to peel it; the skin softens during baking.

Combine the eggs, milk, oil, and horseradish in a large mixing bowl and beat together. Add the flour, cheese, and apple. Season with salt and pepper, and stir to combine. Gently fold in the baking powder.

Transfer to the prepared pan and bake for about 50 minutes. Let cool in the pan before turning out.

Variation  Use 7 oz (200 g) grated pumpkin instead of the apple.

## MUSTARD CAKE

Preparation time: 10 minutes
Cooking time: 50 minutes

**small bunch of fresh tarragon**
**3 eggs**
**6 Tbsp (3½ fl oz/100 mL) low-fat milk**
**6 Tbsp (3½ fl oz/100 mL) vegetable oil**
**2 Tbsp coarsegrain mustard**
**1¾ cups (7 oz/200 g) flour**
**1¼ cups (3½ oz/100 g) grated cheese, such as mild cheddar**
**1 Tbsp baking powder**
**salt, pepper**

Preheat the oven to 350°F (180°C). Butter and flour a cake pan.

Finely chop the tarragon.

In a large mixing bowl, combine the eggs, milk, oil, and mustard and beat together. Add the flour, cheese, and tarragon. Season with salt and pepper, and stir to combine. Gently fold in the baking powder.

Transfer to the prepared pan and bake for about 50 minutes. Let cool in the pan before turning out. Slice when completely cooled.

OPPY SEED CORNMEAL CAKE * CORN AND CHO

RICOTS AND HAZELNUTS * FIG AND CINNAMON C

ESAME SEEDS * POPPY SEED CAKE * CHOCOLATE CH

IVE, THYME, AND LEMON * POPPY SEED CORNMEAL

OLIVE CAKE * DRY APRICOTS AND HAZELNUTS

GS AND ROSEMARY * SESAME SEEDS * POPPY S

MON * POPPY SEED CORNMEAL CAKE * CORN AND

ZO * OLIVE CAKE * BACON AND ONION CAKE * D|

* RAISINS AND WALNUTS * FIGS AND ROSEMARY

* CAKES THAT THINK THEY'RE BREAD *

KE * CORN AND CHORIZO * BACON AND ONION CA|

FIG AND CINNAMON CAKE * RAISINS AND WALNUTS

CAKE * CHOCOLATE CHIPS * OLIVE, THYME, AN

RIZO * BACON AND ONION CAKE...

THESE CAKES ARE IDEAL AT BREAKFAST OR
FOR SUNDAY BRUNCH. SERVE WITH A LITTLE
SALTED BUTTER, SLICED HAM, OR JAM. THESE
CAKES ARE VERY SIMILAR TO BREAD.

## POPPYSEED CORNMEAL CAKE

Preparation time: 10 minutes
Cooking time: 50 minutes

3 eggs
1 cup (8 fl oz/250 mL) buttermilk
5 Tbsp (2½ fl oz/75 mL) vegetable oil
1 heaping cup (7 oz/200 g) cornmeal or fine grade polenta
⅔ cup (3½ oz/100 g) flour
3 Tbsp poppy seeds
1 Tbsp baking powder
salt, pepper

Preheat the oven to 350°F (180°C). Butter and flour
a cake pan.

Combine the eggs, milk, and oil in a large mixing
bowl and beat together. Add the cornmeal, flour,
and poppy seeds. Season with salt and pepper, and
stir to combine. Gently fold in the baking powder.

Transfer to the prepared pan and bake for about
50 minutes. Let cool in the pan before turning out.
To turnout, run the tip of a sharp knife around the
inside of the pan before inverting.

## CORN AND CHORIZO CAKE

Preparation time: 10 minutes
Cooking time: 50 minutes

3½ oz (100 g) chorizo
3 eggs
1 cup (8 fl oz/250 mL) buttermilk
6 Tbsp (3 fl oz/70 mL) vegetable oil
2½ cups (10 oz/300 g) whole-wheat flour
3½ oz (100 g) canned corn, drained
1 Tbsp baking powder
salt, pepper

Preheat the oven to 350°F (180°C). Butter and flour
a cake pan.

Cut the chorizo into thin strips.

Combine the eggs, milk, and oil in a large mixing
bowl and beat together. Add the flour, chorizo, and
corn. Season with salt and pepper, and stir to
combine. Gently fold in the baking powder.

Transfer to the prepared pan and bake for about
50 minutes. Let cool in the pan before turning out.
To turn out, run the tip of a sharp knife around the
inside of the pan before inverting.

## OLIVE, THYME, AND LEMON CAKE

Preparation time: 15 minutes
Cooking time: 50 minutes

3½ oz (100 g) pitted black olives
handful of fresh thyme
3 eggs
¾ cup (7 fl oz/200 ml) buttermilk
6 Tbsp (3½ fl oz/100 mL) olive oil
2½ cups (10 oz/300 g) spelt flour
grated zest of 1 lemon
1 Tbsp baking powder
salt, pepper

Preheat the oven to 350°F (180°C). Butter and flour
a cake pan.

Put the olives in a food processor and chop
coarsely. Strip the thyme leaves from the stems.

Combine the eggs, milk, and oil in a large mixing
bowl and beat together. Add the flour, olives, lemon
zest, and thyme, reserving a few leaves for garnish.
Season with salt and pepper, and stir to combine.
Gently fold in the baking powder.

Transfer to the prepared pan, sprinkle the top with
the reserved thyme leaves and bake for about
50 minutes. Let cool in the pan before turning out.

## BACON AND ONION CAKE

Preparation time: 15 minutes
Cooking time: 50 minutes

1 onion
3 eggs
¾ cup (7 fl oz/200 mL) buttermilk
6 Tbsp (3½ fl oz/100 mL) olive oil
¾ cup (3½ oz/100 g) flour
1⅓ cups (7 oz/200 g) whole-wheat flour
3½ oz (100 g) finely chopped bacon
1 Tbsp baking powder
salt, pepper

Preheat the oven to 350°F (180°C). Butter and flour
a cake pan.

Cut the onion in half and slice thinly. Heat a small
amount of oil in a pan, add the onion slices and
cook until browned. Thinly slice the remaining
onion half and set aside for garnish.

Combine the eggs, milk, and oil in a large mixing
bowl and beat together. Add the flours, bacon, and
browned onions. Season with salt and pepper, and
stir to combine. Gently fold in the baking powder.

Transfer to the prepared pan, arrange the sliced
onions on top and bake for about 50 minutes.
If the onions brown too quickly, cover with a sheet
of aluminum paper. Let cool in the pan before
turning out.

## APRICOT AND HAZELNUT CAKE

Preparation time: 15 minutes
Cooking time: 50 minutes

2 large handfuls of dry apricots
2 large handfuls of whole hazelnuts
3 eggs
1 cup (8 fl oz/250 mL) buttermilk
5 Tbsp (2½ fl oz/75 mL) vegetable or hazelnut oil
1⅓ cups (7 oz/200 g) whole-wheat flour
1 cup (3½ oz/100 g) rolled oats
1 Tbsp baking powder
salt, pepper

Preheat the oven to 350°F (180°C). Butter and flour a cake pan.

Cut the apricots into small cubes. Coarsely chop the hazelnuts.

Combine the eggs, milk, and oil in a large mixing bowl and beat together. Add the flour, oats, apricots, and hazelnuts. Season with salt and pepper, and stir to combine. Gently fold in the baking powder.

Transfer to the prepared pan and bake for about 50 minutes. Let cool in the pan before turning out.

Note  You can crush the hazelnuts using a mortar and pestle.

## RAISIN AND WALNUT CAKE

Preparation time: 10 minutes
Cooking time: 50 minutes

2 large handfuls of raisins
2 large handfuls of coarsely chopped walnut pieces
3 eggs
1 cup (8 fl oz/250 mL) buttermilk
5 Tbsp (2½ fl oz/75 mL) vegetable oil
¾ cup (3½ oz/100 g) flour
1⅓ cups (7 oz/200 g) whole-wheat flour
1 Tbsp baking powder
salt

Preheat the oven to 350°F (180°C). Butter and flour a cake pan.

Combine the eggs, milk, and oil in a large mixing bowl and beat together. Add the flours, raisins, and walnuts. Season with salt, and mix to combine. Gently fold in the baking powder.

Transfer to the prepared pan, arrange the sliced onions on top and bake for about 50 minutes. Let cool in the pan before turning out.

## FIG AND ROSEMARY CAKE

Preparation time: 15 minutes
Cooking time: 50 minutes

2 large handfuls of dry figs
bunch of fresh rosemary
3 eggs
1 cup (8 fl oz/250 mL) buttermilk
5 Tbsp (2½ fl oz/75 mL) vegetable oil
1 cup (5 oz/150 g) whole-wheat flour
1 cup (5 oz/150 g) spelt flour
1 Tbsp baking powder
salt

Preheat the oven to 350°F (180°C). Butter and flour a cake pan.

Cut the figs into small cubes. Strip the rosemary leaves from the stems and chop finely.

Combine the eggs, milk, and oil in a large mixing bowl and beat together. Add the flours, figs, and rosemary. Season with salt, and mix to combine. Gently fold in the baking powder.

Transfer to the prepared pan and bake for about 50 minutes. Let cool in the pan before turning out.

Note  You can decorate the top of the cake with a few figs.

# YUMMY IDEAS

THE CAKES ON THIS PAGE ARE MADE WITH
WHOLE-WHEAT FLOUR AND ARE MORE
SUBSTANTIAL. THEY ARE VERSATILE AND CAN
BE SERVED AT BREAKFAST AS WELL AS WITH
DRINKS. THESE COMBINATIONS ARE BUT A
FEW OF THE MANY WAYS YOU CAN IMPROVISE
ON THE BASIC RECIPE.

## LAYER CAKE

Cut the cake into three layers lengthwise.
Spread each layer with one of the following fillings.
Sandwich the layers back together then wrap
the cake in plastic wrap. Refrigerate for at least
2 hours. Cut into slices to serve.

## MINI SANDWICHES

• Make mini sandwiches using cured ham, some
arugula, and sun-dried tomatoes

• Make canapés using any of the following fillings.

• Make elegant sandwiches for a buffet by slicing
the cake very thinly. Arrange a filling on top
(smoked salmon, curried chicken, pesto spread,
or leftover mixed roasted vegetables). Trim the
edges and cut into three equal pieces.

## QUICK FILLINGS

### Ricotta Cheese and Horseradish

Combine 7 oz (200 g) ricotta cheese with
4–5 Tbsp grated horseradish. Season with salt
and pepper.

### Ricotta Cheese and Pesto

Combine 7 oz (200 g) ricotta cheese with
5 tsp pesto. Season with salt and pepper.

### Tuna, Shallots, Lemon, and Mayonnaise

Drain a 7 oz (200 g) can of tuna packed in water
and chop the shallot finely. In a bowl, combine the
tuna, shallot, 3 Tbsp mayonnaise, and the juice of
1 lemon. Season with salt and pepper.

### Sardine, Quark, and Pickles

Drain a 4 oz (120 g) can of sardines. With a fork,
crush the sardines to a coarse paste. Put them in
a bowl and combine with 3½ oz (100 g) quark or
fromage frais, 3 small dill pickles, very finely
chopped, and 4–6 Tbsp (2–3 fl oz/60–90 mL)
mayonnaise. Add the juice of ½ lemon. Season with
salt and pepper.

### Quark, Cumin Seed, Chive, and Butter

Beat 8 Tbsp softened butter until smooth. Add
3½ oz (100 g) quark or fromage frais and a handful
of chopped chives. Add 1 tsp cumin seed. Season
with salt and pepper.

### Spicy Quark

Mix 3½ oz (100 g) quark or fromage frais with
2 tsp paprika or ground chili. Add a handful of
finely chopped chives. Season with salt and pepper.

### Roquefort, Apple, Walnut, and Butter

Beat 3 Tbsp softened butter until smooth. Crush
3½ oz (100 g) Roquefort with the back of a fork and
add to the butter. Add ½ grated apple and a few
chopped walnuts. Season with salt and pepper.

### Cream Cheese, Radish, and Basil

Finely chop a bunch of trimmed radishes and
combine with 5 oz (150 g) cream cheese. Add a
handful of coarsely chopped basil. Season with
salt and pepper.

### Egg Salad with Fresh Herbs

Finely chop 4 hard-boiled eggs. Add 3–4 Tbsp
mayonnaise, 3½ oz (100 g) cream cheese, a handful
of chopped parsley, and 1 tsp wholegrain mustard.
Season with salt and pepper and mix well.

### Mild Cheddar, Garlic, and Mayonnaise

Finely grate 5 oz (150 g) mild cheddar or Emmental.
Combine with 3–4 crushed garlic cloves and 4–6
Tbsp (3½ fl oz/100 mL) mayonnaise. Season with salt
and pepper.

## CHOCOLATE CHIP CAKE

Preparation time: 10 minutes
Cooking time: 50 minutes

3 eggs
1 cup (8 fl oz/250 mL) buttermilk
5 Tbsp (2½ fl oz/75 mL) vegetable oil
2½ cups (10 oz/300 g) whole-wheat flour
3½ oz (100 g) chocolate chips
1 Tbsp baking powder
salt

Preheat the oven to 350°F (180°C). Butter and flour a cake pan.

Combine the eggs, milk, and oil in a large mixing bowl and beat together. Add the flour and chocolate chips. Season with salt and mix to combine. Gently fold in the baking powder.

Transfer to the prepared pan and bake for about 50 minutes. Let cool in the pan before turning out.

## SESAME SEED CAKE

Preparation time: 10 minutes
Cooking time: 50 minutes

3 Tbsp sesame seeds
3 eggs
1 cup (8 fl oz/250 mL) buttermilk
5 Tbsp (2½ fl oz/75 mL) vegetable oil
⅔ cup (3½ oz/100 g) whole-wheat flour
1⅓ cups (7 oz/200 g) chestnut flour
1 Tbsp baking powder
salt

Preheat the oven to 350°F (180°C). Butter and flour a cake pan.

Heat a small pan and dry-fry the sesame seeds until they begin to smell toasted.

Combine the eggs, milk, and oil in a large mixing bowl and beat together. Add the flours and sesame seeds. Season with salt and mix to combine. Gently fold in the baking powder.

Transfer to the prepared pan and bake for about 50 minutes. Let cool in the pan before turning out.

## FIG AND CINNAMON CAKE

Preparation time: 15 minutes
Cooking time: 50 minutes

5 oz (150 g) fresh ripe figs
3 eggs
1 cup (8 fl oz/250 mL) buttermilk
5 Tbsp (2½ fl oz/75 mL) vegetable oil
1 cup (5 oz/150 g) whole-wheat flour
1 cup (5 oz/150 g) spelt flour
1 tsp ground cinnamon
1 Tbsp baking powder
salt

Preheat the oven to 350°F (180°C). Butter and flour a cake pan.

Chop the figs coarsely.

Combine the eggs, milk, and oil in a large mixing bowl and beat together. Add the flours, figs, and cinnamon. Season with salt and mix to combine. Gently fold in the baking powder.

Transfer to the prepared pan and bake for about 50 minutes. If the cake browns too quickly, cover the top with a sheet of aluminum foil. Let cool in the pan before turning out.

CAKE * RASPBERRY AND ALMOND PASTE CAKE * PECAN
PRUNE, WALNUT, AND CINNAMON CAKE * ALMOND P.
BLUEBERRY AND LEMON * ALMOND CHICORY CAKE *
PEPPER CAKE * CHOCOLATE CHIP AND PEAR CAKE *
HONEY AND PINE NUT CAKE * MANGO VANILLA
AND ZUCCHINI CAKE * POPPY SEED CAKE * GREE
MARMALADE CAKE * IRISH WHISKEY CAKE * STRIPY C
FRUIT * CHOCOLATE, BASIL, AND PEPPER * PISTACH
FRUIT CAKE * PISTACHIO AND LEMON CAKE * SPIC
APPLE, CARROT, AND ALMOND CAKE * CHOCOLATE LIC
CANDIED CHESTNUTS * BANANA AND WALNUT CAKE *
DOUBLE CHOCOLATE CAKE * RASPBERRY
GINGER CAKE * CANDIED FRUIT * PRUNE, WALNUT, A
AND WALNUT CAKE * LEMON CURD * BLUEBERRY AND
ANISEED * STRAWBERRY, PISTACHIO, AND PEPPER CA
CLOVE * CRYSTALIZED ROSE PETALS * HONEY
CAKE WITH FIGS AND APRICOTS * APPLE AND ZUC
WHITE CHOCOLATE CAKE * ORANGE MARMALADE
ALMOND * LEMON CURD * CHOCOLATE-COATED FR
AND LEMON CAKE * IRISH WHISKY * ORCHARD FRUIT
WITH APPLE AND PEAR * PINK RHUBARB CAKE * APPLE,
PLUM AND HAZELNUT * FRESH FIG AND CANDIED
HONEY PINEAPPLE CAKE * CRUSHED FRUIT CREAM

CAKE * CRUSHED FRUIT CREAM * DOUBLE CHOCOLA

KE * PEAR AND GINGER CAKE * CANDIED FRUI

E * APPLE, RAISIN, AND WALNUT CAKE * LEMON CUR

AR AND ANISEED * STRAWBERRY, PISTACHIO, AN

UMPKIN AND CLOVE * CRYSTALIZED ROSE PETALS

E * SPICE CAKE WITH FIGS AND APRICOTS * APPL

EA AND WHITE CHOCOLATE CAKE * ORAN

OLATE ALMOND * LEMON CURD * CHOCOLATE-COATE

AND LEMON CAKE * SWEET CAKES * ORCHAR

AKE WITH APPLE AND PEAR * PINK RHUBARB CAKE

UR * PLUM AND HAZELNUT * FRESH FIG AN

AME-HONEY PINEAPPLE CAKE * CRUSHED FRUIT CREA

ALMOND PASTE CAKE * PECAN CAKE * PEAR AN

CINNAMON CAKE * ALMOND PASTE * APPLE, RAISI

MON * ALMOND CHICORY CAKE * PEAR AN

* CHOCOLATE CHIP AND PEAR CAKE * PUMPKIN AN

D PINE NUT CAKE * MANGO VANILLA CAKE * SPIC

NI CAKE * POPPY SEED CAKE * GREEN TEA AN

CAKE * IRISH WHISKEY CAKE * STRIPY CHOCOLAT

* CHOCOLATE, BASIL, AND PEPPER * PISTACHI

E * PISTACHIO AND LEMON CAKE * SPICE CAK

RROT, AND ALMOND CAKE * CHOCOLATE LIQUEU

HESTNUTS * BANANA AND WALNUT CAKE * SESAME

OUBLE CHOCOLATE CAKE * RASPBERRY AND ALMON

# THE TWO BASIC RECIPES

I USE TWO BASIC RECIPES IN THIS BOOK. THE FIRST IS A POUND CAKE, WHICH I HAVE MODIFIED SLIGHTLY BY REDUCING THE AMOUNTS OF SUGAR AND BUTTER. THIS RECIPE CAN BE SERVED JUST AS IT IS.
THE SECOND IS A MUFFIN RECIPE USING OIL INSTEAD OF BUTTER AND BUTTERMILK, WHICH GIVES THE FINISHED CAKE A PLEASANT TANG. IF YOU PREFER, YOU CAN REPLACE THE BUTTERMILK WITH LOW-FAT MILK, YOGURT, OR CRÈME FRAÎCHE.

## LIGHT BASIC POUND CAKE

Preparation time: 10 minutes
Cooking time: 40 minutes

**5 oz (150 g) butter**
**3 eggs**
**¾ cup + 2 Tbsp (6 oz/175 g) sugar**
**1½ cups (6 oz/175 g) flour**
**½ Tbsp baking powder**
**pinch of salt**

Melt the butter in a microwave or in a bowl set over a pan of simmering water.

Beat the eggs and sugar in a large mixing bowl until light and frothy. Add the flour, salt, butter, and baking powder.

## MUFFIN CAKE

Preparation time: 10 minutes
Cooking time: 40 minutes

**2 eggs**
**¾ cup (7 fl oz/200 mL) buttermilk**
**6 Tbsp (3½ fl oz/100 mL) vegetable oil**
**2½ cups (10 oz/300 g) flour**
**¾ cup + 2 Tbsp (6 oz/175 g) sugar**
**½ Tbsp baking powder**
**pinch of salt**

Beat together the eggs, milk, and oil. Then add in the flour, salt, sugar, and baking powder.

This recipe is ideal for individual cakes because it is very moist, but it is equally suited to regular cake pans.

## FLOUR

Some of the flour can be replaced with ground almonds, walnuts, or hazelnuts, as well as with oatmeal (polenta flour) or other grains.

## SUGAR

Replace ordinary sugar with raw sugar or light brown sugar.

## STORE CUPBOARD INGREDIENTS

Experiment with ingredients you may already have in your cupboard. And don't stick to the tried and tested regulars like dry or candied fruit. Be bold and try unusual combinations or unexpected ingredients, say instant coffee or chicory, honey, spices and herbs...

## FRUIT

When baking with fruit, it is always best to use fresh. Frozen fruit are not as flavorful, nor do they hold their shape well. If you do go for frozen fruit, be sure to defrost completely before using and be sure they are not too soft or they will reduce to a purée in your batter.

## HERBS AND SPICES

Go right ahead and add some herbs and spices to your sweet cakes: any kind of peppercorn, turmeric, cardamom, basil, thyme... Contrary to popular belief, herbs and spices go remarkably well with sweet things.

## ALCOHOL

Unless you are serving cake to children, alcohol is a fabulous flavoring ingredient. Try rum, brandy, or anise-flavored spirits such as pastis. Add them straight to the batter, or use to moisten the cake immediately after cooking.

## MY DISCOVERIES

To help you along in your culinary explorations, here are a few of my favorite combinations:

Chocolate/Pepper
Lemon/Thyme
Strawberry/Pepper
Rhubarb/Cardamom
Turmeric/Ginger
Anise/Chocolate

The sweet cake kit

flour

eggs

sugar

butter

milk

salt + dry fruit

# LITTLE THINGS THAT MAKE A DIFFERENCE

YOU CAN DECIDE WHETHER YOU PREFER WHITE
OR BROWN SUGAR, CANDIED OR DRY FRUIT…
THE IMPORTANT THING IS, ALWAYS CHOOSE
THE BEST INGREDIENTS.

## SUGAR

**Regular or superfine**

This gives a light texture.

**Confectioner's sugar**

This is made from sugar crystals that have been
ground very finely. It can be dusted over the tops
of finished cakes, used for meringues, and also
used for icing. It must be stored in a cool dry place
to prevent lumps from forming.

**Raw sugar**

This is obtained directly from sugar cane juice and
has a darker color and more intense flavor, slightly
reminiscent of rum. It lends a distinctive taste to
sweet cakes.

**Brown sugar**

This is refined sugar with a soft, sticky texture,
darker color and more pronounced flavor. Use it in
place of white sugar when baking cakes. Store in an
airtight container.

## DRY FRUIT

Soft fruit are best for cakes: apricots, figs, prunes,
apples, pears, bananas, dates, papayas, and raisins.
The choice is vast.

Rehydrate dry fruit by soaking them in alcohol,
fruit juice, tea, or herbal tea. They will absorb
flavors readily. It is always best to leave dry fruit to
soak for several hours at least, or even overnight.
If you are short on time, soften in the microwave.
Simply heat the fruit on High for 2–3 minutes.

Dry fruit go well with all kinds of nuts (walnuts,
pecans, almonds, hazelnuts), with grated fresh
fruit, and with vegetables.

## CANDIED FRUIT

Large stores should stock an assortment of
candied fruit such as Maraschino cherries, citrus
peel, and sometimes angelica. Specialty stores are
another good source of candied fruit and the
quality and selection is often superior.

## NUTS

**Almonds**

Almonds are sold in a variety of forms: blanched
(skins removed), whole, slivered, chopped, ground,
or as almond paste (marzipan). Always buy
almonds in small quantities as they quickly lose
their freshness.

To blanch almonds at home, simply plunge whole,
shelled almonds into boiling water for 2 minutes.
Remove and use your thumb and forefinger
to squeeze the white almond out of its dark
outer skin.

Toasted almonds are even more flavorful. To toast
almonds yourself, dry-fry in a small non-stick pan
until they are just brown.

**Walnuts**

For ground walnuts, put walnut pieces in a food
processor and pulse. For an even richer taste,
dry-fry the walnuts in a non-stick pan before
grinding. Walnuts have a very short shelf life and
are best kept in an airtight container or even in
the refrigerator.

**Hazelnuts**

For ground hazelnuts, put the hazelnuts in a food
processor and pulse. For an even richer taste,
dry-fry the hazelnuts in a non-stick pan before
grinding them.

**Pine nuts and pistachios**

Pine nuts are the small white grains extracted
from a certain species of pine tree, found mainly
around the Mediterranean. They are easily
obtainable in large stores.

Pistachios are used ground or halved. Their
attractive green color makes them useful as an
ingredient and for decoration.

RAW SUGAR

BROWN SUGAR

FRESH FRUIT

DRY FRUIT

CANDIED FRUIT

NUTS

PINE NUTS

PISTACHIOS

# DECORATING

SOMETIMES IT'S HARD TO COME UP WITH AN ORIGINAL IDEA, AND EVEN HARDER TO FIND INSPIRATION. DON'T KNOCK YOURSELF OUT; ORIGINAL DOESN'T HAVE TO MEAN COMPLICATED. HERE ARE SOME SIMPLE IDEAS.

### MY TIPS FOR DECORATING

If you are short of ideas, look for inspiration around you. Flick through a magazine or book, check out the bakery section, or visit a specialty bakery. There is always something you will like. You do not necessarily have to copy an idea exactly, simply find a few decorative elements that appeal and combine them into something uniquely yours. Sometimes you do not need much more than some colored sugar, silver balls, or sugar flowers.

### OUT OF THE ORDINARY IDEAS

For even more flavor, enhance your cakes by moistening them with syrups or alcohols. Here are a few ideas.

### FLAVORED SYRUP

**2 cups (1 pint/500 mL) water**
**1¼ cups (½ lb/250 g) sugar**
**6–8 Tbsp (3½–5 fl oz/100–150 ml) alcohol of your choice**

Heat the water in a pan. Add the sugar and cook for 2 minutes. Remove from the heat and let cool.

To flavor the syrup, add an alcohol: rum, whisky, kirsch, or fruit eau-de-vie (fruit brandy). Allow about 6–8 Tbsp according to taste.

### EGG LIQUEUR

**4 egg yolks**
**1 can (14 oz/397 g) sweetened condensed milk**
**1 can (14 oz/397 g) unsweetened condensed milk**
**2 cups (1 pint/500 mL) rum or vodka**

Combine the eggs and condensed milks. Add the rum or vodka. Transfer to a clean bottle and keep refrigerated.

### CHOCOLATE LIQUEUR

**¾ cup (7 fl oz/200 mL) water**
**¾ cup (5 oz/150 g) sugar**
**2 cups (1 pint/500 mL) milk**
**3½ oz (100 g) dark chocolate, broken into pieces**
**1¼ cups (10 fl oz/300 mL) rum**

Heat the water in a pan. Add the sugar and cook for 2 minutes. In another pan, heat the milk. Add the chocolate and melt. Remove from the heat and let cool. Add the rum and stir well. Transfer to a clean bottle and keep refrigerated.

### RASPBERRY LIQUEUR

**½ lb (250g) raspberries**
**2 cups (1 pint/500 mL) eau-de-vie (fruit brandy)**
**2 cups (1 pint/500 mL) water**
**¾ cup + 2 Tbsp (6 oz/175 g) sugar**

One month in advance, combine the raspberries and eau-de-vie (fruit brandy) and leave to macerate. Two to three days before using, heat the water in a pan, add the sugar and cook for 2 minutes. Let cool. Add to the raspberry mixture. Transfer to a clean bottle.

### CRUSHED FRUIT CREAM

**1 cup (7 oz/200 g) crème fraîche**
**2 Tbsp confectioner's sugar**
**¼ lb (125g) fresh soft fruit (raspberries, passion fruit, strawberries, etc)**

In a bowl, whip the crème fraîche until just firm, then gradually add in the sugar. Stir in the fruit that has been coarsely crushed. Spread cream over the cake.

Variation  Use mascarpone in place of the whipped cream, or use equal amounts of both.

# DECORATION

ICING CAN IMPROVE THE APPEARANCE OF
A CAKE AS WELL AS HELP IT TO STAY
FRESHER LONGER.

## LEMON ICING

**1¼ cups (5 oz/150 g) confectioner's sugar**
**1 Tbsp very hot water**
**3 Tbsp lemon juice**

Combine the sugar, water, and lemon juice, stirring
until smooth and shiny. Use immediately.

## VARIATIONS

- **Orange icing**

Use orange juice instead of the lemon juice.

- **Coffee icing**

Use strong black coffee instead of the lemon juice

- **Milk icing**

Use milk instead of water and omit the lemon juice.

- **Cream icing**

Use pouring cream in place of the water and omit
the lemon juice.

- **Rum icing**

Use a splash of rum and a little less water.

- **Red icing**

Replace the water with grenadine syrup.

## HOMEMADE ALMOND PASTE

**1 egg white**
**1 cup (3½ oz/100 g) ground almonds**
**¾ cup 3½ oz/100 g) confectioner's sugar**
**few drops almond extract**

In a bowl, lightly beat the egg white with a fork. In
another bowl, combine the almonds and sugar.
Gradually add the egg white. Blend to obtain a
smooth paste that does not stick to your fingers.
If the mixture is too thin, add more sugar; if it is
too thick, add more egg white. Almond paste will
keep in the refrigerator, covered, for several days.

## CRYSTALIZED ROSE PETALS

**petals from 1 untreated rose**
**1 egg white, beaten**
**confectioner's sugar for dusting**

Dip the rose petals in egg white then dust with
sugar. Set aside to dry for at least 1 hour.

Variation  Replace the rose petals with soft fruit
such as red currants, cherries, raspberries, blackcurrant,
strawberries, or small apricots. For a truly stunning
decoration, keep the stems on and crystalize the
whole fruit.

## CHOCOLATE-COATED FRUIT

**2 oz (60 g) dark or white chocolate**
**1 tsp vegetable oil**
**fruit of your choice**

Melt the chocolate with the oil. Dip the fruit into
the melted chocolate and set aside to harden for
30 minutes. You can decorate the fruit with the
icing of your choice.

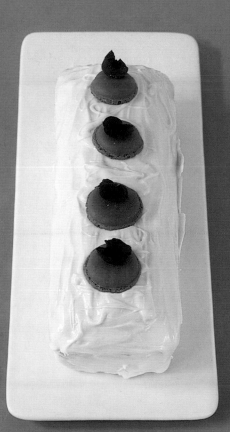

# FRUIT COULIS AND OTHER SAUCES

HERE ARE A FEW SUGGESTIONS TO ACCOMPANY
YOUR SWEET CAKES. TRY THEM, THEY ARE ALL
DELICIOUS!

## FRUIT COULIS

½ lb (250 g) soft fruit, such as raspberries, strawberries,
mangoes, kiwi, etc.
1–2 Tbsp vanilla sugar

Blend the fruit in a food processor and season to
taste with the sugar.

## LEMON CURD

Zest and juice of 2 large lemons
1 cup (7 oz/200 g) sugar
6 Tbsp (3 oz/90 g) butter
3 eggs

Combine all the ingredients in a heatproof bowl
and mix well. Set over a pan of simmering water
and cook, stirring often, until thick.

## REDCURRANT CURD

This is the same as Lemon Curd, but made with
tart redcurrants.

½ lb (250 g) redcurrants, fresh or frozen
1 cup (7 oz/200 g) sugar
juice of 1 lemon
6 Tbsp (3 oz/90 g) butter
3 eggs

In a pan, combine the redcurrants with some water
and cook until softened. Add the sugar, lemon,
butter, and eggs. Transfer to a heatproof bowl and
set over a pan of simmering water and cook,
stirring constantly, until thick.

Variation  Many other fruits can be used in place of the
redcurrants, such as passion fruit, cranberries,
gooseberries, etc.

Tip  Most cakes are always better 24 hours after
they have been made so, if you can, make them
in advance.

## LEMON CURD CAKE

Preparation time: 15 minutes
Cooking time: 50 minutes

12 Tbsp (6 oz/175 g) butter
3 eggs
3/4 cup (5½ oz/160 g) sugar
1½ cups (6 oz/175 g) flour
1 tsp ground cinnamon
½ Tbsp baking powder
1 pot of lemon curd (see left)
pinch of salt

Preheat the oven to 350°F (180°C). Butter and flour
a cake pan.

Melt the butter in a microwave or in a bowl set
over a pan of simmering water.

Whisk the eggs and sugar in a large mixing bowl
until light and frothy. Gradually add the flour, salt,
and melted butter. Stir in the cinnamon and mix
well. Gently fold in the baking powder.

Transfer to the prepared pan and bake for
50 minutes. Let cool completely before turning out.

Slice the cake into 3 layers lengthwise and spread
each layer with some lemon curd. Reassemble
the layers and refrigerate for at least 1 hour
before serving.

## HONEY AND PINE NUT CAKE

Preparation time: 10 minutes
Cooking time: 40 minutes

2 eggs
⅓ cup (3½ oz/100 g) brown sugar
6 Tbsp (3½ fl oz/100 ml) vegetable oil
4 heaping tablespoons (5 oz/150 g) honey
½ cup (4 fl oz/125 ml) buttermilk
2 cups (½ lb/250 g) flour
100 g pine nuts
½ teaspoon ground cinnamon
handful of thyme or rosemary leaves, chopped (optional)
½ Tbsp baking powder
½ tsp baking soda (optional)
pinch of salt

Preheat the oven to 350°F (180°C). Butter and flour a cake pan.

Finely chop the thyme.

Lightly beat the eggs with the sugar, oil, honey, and milk in a large mixing bowl. Gradually add the flour, salt, pine nuts, cinnamon, and thyme and blend everything lightly until just combined without overmixing. Gently fold in the baking powder and the baking soda.

Transfer to the prepared pan and bake for 40 minutes. Let cool slightly before turning out.

Tip  If you don't have any buttermilk, use regular milk acidulated with a few drops of lemon juice, or use crème fraîche. You can use chopped pistachio nuts instead of the pine nuts.

## PECAN CAKE

Preparation time: 10 minutes
Cooking time: 40 minutes

1¼ cups (6 oz/175 g) flour
1 egg
3 Tbsp maple syrup
¼ cup (2 oz/60 g) sugar
8 Tbsp (¼ lb/125 g) butter
7 fl oz (200 ml) crème fraîche
handful of shelled pecans
½ Tbsp baking powder
pinch of salt

Preheat the oven to 350°F (180°C). Butter and flour a cake pan.

Melt the butter in the microwave or in a bowl set over a pan of simmering water. Roughly chop the pecans.

Whisk together the eggs, maple syrup, sugar, crème fraîche, and melted butter in a large mixing bowl. Add the flour, pecans, and salt and stir until just combined without overmixing. Gently fold in the baking powder.

Transfer to the prepared pan and bake for about 40 minutes. Let cool slightly before turning out.

## TRADITIONAL CAKE

Soaking time: 1 hour
Preparation time: 20 minutes
Cooking time: 40 minutes

½ lb (250 g) raisins (use a variety of raisins if you can)
3½ oz (100 g) candied citrus peel (orange, mandarine, lemon)
3½ oz (100 g) candied cherries
3 Tbsp rum or brandy
¾ cup + 2 Tbsp (7 oz/200 g) brown sugar
14 Tbsp (7 oz/200 g) butter, softened
3 eggs
2 cups (½ lb/250 g) flour
3½ oz (100 g) chopped hazelnuts or walnuts
zest of 1 untreated lemon
pinch of ground cinnamon
½ tsp ground Sichuan or Jamaican peppercorns
1 Tbsp baking powder
pinch of salt

Place the dry fruits and the candied fruits in a bowl and pour over the rum. Leave to macerate for up to 1 hour.

Preheat the oven to 350°F (180°C). Butter and flour a cake pan.

Cream the butter and the sugar in a large mixing bowl. Add in the eggs, one at a time, the flour, salt, dry fruits and their soaking liquor, nuts, lemon zest, and spices. Stir until just combined without overmixing. Gently fold in the baking powder.

Transfer to the prepared pan and bake for about 40 minutes. Let cool slightly before turning out.

## DRIED BANANA AND WALNUT CAKE

Preparation time: 15 minutes
Cooking time: 40 minutes

3 eggs
1 cup (5 oz/150 g) brown sugar
6 Tbsp (3½ fl oz/100 mL) vegetable oil
1¼ cups (6 oz/175 g) whole-wheat flour
3½ oz (100 g) dried bananas, chopped
2 handfuls of chopped walnuts
½ Tbsp baking powder
pinch of salt

Preheat the oven to 350°F (180°C). Butter and flour a cake pan.

Whisk together the eggs, sugar, and oil in a large mixing bowl. Add the flour, salt, bananas, and walnuts and stir until just combined without overmixing. Gently fold in the baking powder.

Transfer to the prepared pan and bake for about 40 minutes.

Variation  Use dates instead of bananas and add 2–3 Tbsp rum.

## SPICE CAKE WITH FIGS AND APRICOTS

Soaking time: 1 hour
Preparation time: 15 minutes
Cooking time: 40 minutes

2 handfuls of dried figs
2 handfuls of dried apricots
2 handfuls of raisins
zest of 1 lemon
zest of ½ orange
3 Tbsp rum
3 Tbsp (1½ oz/50 g) butter
3 eggs
¼ cup (1 oz/30 g) confectioner's sugar
6 Tbsp (3½ fl oz/100 mL) low-fat milk
4 heaping Tbsp (5 oz/150 g) honey
1¼ cups (5 oz/150 g) chestnut flour
¾ cup (3½ oz/100 g) flour
2 handfuls of hazelnuts
1 tsp ground allspice
1 Tbsp baking powder
pinch of salt

Soak the figs, apricots, raisins, and zests in the rum for 1 hour.

Preheat the oven to 350°F (180°C). Butter and flour a cake pan. Melt the butter in a microwave or in a bowl set over a pan of simmering water.

Beat together the eggs and sugar in a large mixing bowl until light, fluffy, and doubled in volume. Add the milk, honey, flours, salt, and butter. Stir in the fruit and the rum, the hazelnuts, allspice, and baking powder.

Transfer to the prepared pan and bake for about 40 minutes.

## SPICE CAKE WITH APPLE AND PEAR

Soaking time: 1 hour
Preparation time: 20 minutes
Cooking time: 40 minutes

2 handfuls of dried apples, chopped
2 handfuls of dried pears, chopped
2 handfuls of raisins
zest of ½ orange
3 Tbsp calvados (apple brandy)
6 Tbsp (3½ fl oz/100 mL) low-fat milk
5 heaping Tbsp (6 oz/175 g) honey
3 eggs
¼ cup (1 oz/30 g) confectioner's sugar
1 cup (4½ oz/140 g) rye flour
5 Tbsp (2 oz/60 g) flour
3 Tbsp (1¾ oz/50 g) butter, melted
2 handfuls of chopped walnuts
1 tsp ground allspice
1 Tbsp baking powder
pinch of salt

Soak the apples, pears, raisins, and orange zest in the calvados for 1 hour.

Heat the milk in a small pan. Add the honey and stir to dissolve.

Preheat the oven to 350°F (180°C). Butter and flour a cake pan.

Beat together the eggs and sugar in a large mixing bowl until light, fluffy, and doubled in volume. Add the milk mixture, flours, salt, and butter. Stir in the dry fruit and the calvados, the walnuts, allspice, and baking powder.

Transfer to the prepared pan and bake for about 40 minutes.

## PRUNE, WALNUT, AND CINNAMON CAKE

Preparation time: 15 minutes
Cooking time: 40 minutes

5 oz (150 g) prunes
3 Tbsp rum
2 handfuls of walnuts
2 eggs
1 cup (5 oz/150 g) brown sugar
6 Tbsp (3½ fl oz/100 mL) vegetable oil
1 pot (4 fl oz/115 g) set plain yogurt
2 cups (½ lb/250 g) flour
½ tsp ground cinnamon
½ Tbsp baking powder
pinch of salt

Preheat the oven to 350°F (180°C). Butter and flour a cake pan.

Combine three-quarters of the prunes and the rum in a food processor. Mix to obtain a paste. Chop together the remaining prunes and the walnuts.

Beat together the eggs and sugar in a large mixing bowl until light, fluffy, and doubled in volume. Add the oil, prune paste, and yogurt. Stir in the flour, salt, cinnamon, the chopped prunes, and the walnuts. Combine until just blended. Gently fold in the baking powder.

Transfer to the prepared pan and bake for about 40 minutes.

## POPPYSEED CAKE

Preparation time: 10 minutes
Cooking time: 40 minutes

2 eggs
1 cup (¼ lb/125 g) confectioner's sugar
2 cups (½ lb/250 g) flour
6 oz (175g) poppy seeds
½ cup (4½ fl oz/125 mL) low-fat milk
zest of 1 untreated lemon
8 Tbsp (¼ lb/125 g) butter
½ Tbsp baking powder
pinch of salt

Preheat the oven to 350°F (180°C). Butter and flour a cake pan.

Melt the butter in a microwave or in a bowl set over a pan of simmering water and set aside.

Beat the eggs and sugar in a large mixing bowl until light, fluffy, and doubled in volume. Gradually add the flour, salt, poppy seeds, milk, lemon zest, and melted butter. Gently fold in the baking powder.

Transfer to the prepared pan and bake for about 40 minutes. Let cool in the pan slightly before turning out.

## LEMON POPPYSEED CAKE

Preparation time: 15 minutes
Cooking time: 40 minutes

10 Tbsp (5 oz/150 g) butter
juice of 2 lemons
zest of 1 lemon
3 eggs
¾ cup + 2 Tbsp (6 oz/175 g) sugar
1½ cups (6 oz/175 g) flour
1 Tbsp poppy seeds
½ Tbsp baking powder
pinch of salt

Preheat the oven to 350°F (180°C). Butter and flour a cake pan.

Melt the butter in a microwave or in a bowl set over a pan of simmering water and set aside. Wash the lemons. Grate the zest of 1 lemon and squeeze the juice from both.

Beat together the eggs and sugar in a large mixing bowl until light, fluffy, and doubled in volume. Gradually add the flour, salt, poppy seeds, lemon juice and zest, and melted butter. Gently fold in the baking powder.

Transfer to the prepared pan and bake for about 40 minutes. Let cool in the pan slightly before turning out.

## SESAME–HONEY PINEAPPLE CAKE

Preparation time: 15 minutes
Cooking time: 40 minutes

8 Tbsp (¼ lb/125 g) butter
3 eggs
3½ oz (100 g) sesame-honey snack bars
5 oz (150 g) pineapple, fresh or frozen
½ cup (3½ oz/100 g) sugar
1½ cups (6 oz/175 g) flour
½ Tbsp baking powder
pinch of salt

Preheat the oven to 350°F (180°C). Butter and flour a cake pan.

Melt the butter in a microwave or in a bowl set over a pan of simmering water and set aside. Break the sesame-honey bars into small pieces. If using fresh pineapple, cut into small pieces. If using frozen, defrost and cut into small pieces.

Beat together the eggs and sugar in a large mixing bowl until light, fluffy, and doubled in volume. Gradually add the flour, salt, and melted butter. Add the sesame-honey bars and pineapple, stir until just combined without overmixing. Gently fold in the baking powder.

Transfer to the prepared pan and bake for about 40 minutes. Let cool in the pan slightly before turning out.

Note  Use peanut butter brittle in place of the sesame-honey bars.

WITH SO MANY DIFFERENT FRUIT TO CHOOSE
FROM, YOU ARE SURE TO FIND SOMETHING
TO DELIGHT EVERYONE.

## PINK RHUBARB CAKE

Preparation time: 15 minutes
Cooking time: 50 minutes

**10 Tbsp (5 oz/150 g) butter**
**2–3 rhubarb stalks**
**4 cardamom pods**
**3 eggs**
**¾ cup + 2 Tbsp (6 oz/175 g) sugar**
**1½ cups (6 oz/175 g) flour**
**½ Tbsp baking powder**
**pinch of salt**

Preheat the oven to 350°F (180°C). Butter and flour
a cake pan.

Melt the butter in a microwave or in a bowl set
over a pan of simmering water and set aside.
Cut half of one rhubarb stalk into 1-inch (2.5 cm)
pieces; reserve for decoration. Cut the remaining
rhubarb into small pieces. Do not peel the rhubarb
as its outer layer gives the cake its pink color.
Grind the cardamom to a powder with a mortar
and pestle.

Beat together the eggs and sugar in a large mixing
bowl until light, fluffy, and doubled in volume.
Gradually add the flour, salt, and melted butter.
Add the rhubarb and cardamom, stir until just
combined without overmixing. Gently fold in the
baking powder.

Transfer to the prepared pan and distribute the
reserved rhubarb over the top. Bake for about
50 minutes. Let cool in the pan slightly before
turning out.

## RASPBERRY AND ALMOND PASTE CAKE

Preparation time: 15 minutes
Cooking time: 40 minutes

3 eggs
1 cup (5 oz/150 g) raw sugar
10 Tbsp (5 oz/150 g) butter
1½ cups (6 oz/175 g) flour
3½ oz (100 g) almond paste, cut into pieces
5 oz (150 g) raspberries, fresh or frozen
½ Tbsp baking powder
pinch of salt

Preheat the oven to 350°F (180°C). Butter and flour a cake pan.

Melt the butter in a microwave or in a bowl set over a pan of simmering water and set aside

Beat together the eggs and sugar in a large mixing bowl until light, fluffy, and doubled in volume. Gradually add the flour, salt, melted butter, and almond paste. Using a wooden spoon, fold in the raspberries, taking care not to crush them. Gently fold in the baking powder.

Transfer to the prepared pan and bake for about 40 minutes. Let cool in the pan slightly before turning out.

## MIRABELLE CAKE

Preparation time: 20 minutes
Cooking time: 40 minutes

2 eggs
¾ + 2 Tbsp (6 oz/175 g) raw sugar
¾ cup (7 fl oz/200 mL) buttermilk
6 Tbsp (3½ fl oz/100 mL) vegetable oil
1½ cups (6 oz/200 g) flour
¾ cup (3½ oz/100 g) oatmeal
7 oz (200 g) pitted mirabelles or small golden plums, quartered
¼ tsp ground cinnamon
½ Tbsp baking powder
pinch of salt

For the crumble topping
⅓ cup (2 oz/60 g) flour
6 Tbsp ground almonds
3 Tbsp (2 oz/60 g) butter, chilled and diced
3 Tbsp (1½ oz/40 g) sugar

Preheat the oven to 350°F (180°C). Butter and flour a cake pan.

For the crumble, combine all the ingredients in a bowl and mix well with your fingertips until blended and the mixture resembles coarse crumbs.

Beat the eggs, sugar, milk, and oil in a large mixing bowl. Add the flour, oatmeal, salt, mirabelles, and cinnamon. Stir until just combined without overmixing. Gently fold in the baking powder.

Transfer to the prepared pan and sprinkle over the crumble topping. Bake for 20 minutes, then cover with aluminum foil to keep the crumble from burning and cook for a further 20 minutes. Let cool in the pan slightly before turning out.

## PLUM AND HAZELNUT CAKE

Preparation time: 20 minutes
Cooking time: 40 minutes

2 eggs
¾ cup + 2 Tbsp (6 oz/175 g) sugar
¾ cup (7 fl oz/200 mL) buttermilk
6 Tbsp (3½ fl oz/100 mL) vegetable oil
1¼ cups (7 oz/200 g) flour
1 cup (3½ oz/100 g) ground hazelnuts
7 oz (200 g) pitted small red plums, sliced
handful of whole hazelnuts, chopped
½ Tbsp baking powder
pinch of salt

For the crumble topping
¾ cup (3½ oz/100 g) flour
3 Tbsp (2 oz/60 g) butter, chilled and diced
3 Tbsp (1¼ oz/40 g) sugar

Preheat the oven to 350°F (180°C). Butter and flour a cake pan.

For the crumble, combine all the ingredients in a bowl and mix well with your fingertips until blended and the mixture resembles coarse crumbs.

Beat the eggs, sugar, milk, and oil in a large bowl. Add the flour, ground hazelnuts, salt, plums, and chopped hazelnuts. Stir until just combined without overmixing. Gently fold in the baking powder.

Transfer to the prepared pan and sprinkle over the crumble topping. Bake for 20 minutes, then cover with aluminum foil to keep the crumble from burning and cook for a further 20 minutes. Let cool in the pan slightly before turning out.

## STRAWBERRY, PISTACHIO, AND PEPPER CAKE

Preparation time: 15 minutes
Cooking time: 40 minutes

3 eggs
¾ cup + 2 Tbsp (6 oz/175 g) sugar
10 Tbsp (5 oz/150g) butter
1½ cups (6 oz/175 g) flour
¼ tsp ground Sichuan pepper
handful of shelled pistachios, chopped
½ Tbsp baking powder
5 oz (150 g) strawberries, hulled and halved
pinch of salt

Preheat the oven to 350°F (180°C). Butter and flour a cake pan.

Melt the butter in a microwave or in a bowl set over a pan of simmering water and set aside

Beat together the eggs and sugar in a large bowl until light, fluffy, and doubled in volume. Gradually add the flour, salt, melted butter, Sichuan pepper, and pistachios. Gently fold in the baking powder.

Transfer to the prepared pan and bake for about 20 minutes. Arrange the strawberries on top and return to the oven for a further 20 minutes. Let cool in the pan slightly before turning out.

Note  Do not cut the strawberries too small or they lose their shape during cooking.

## FRESH FIG AND CANDIED CHESTNUTS

Preparation time: 15 minutes
Cooking time: 40 minutes

**10 Tbsp (5 oz/150 g) butter**
**5 oz (150 g) fresh figs**
**5 oz (150 g) candied chestnut pieces**
**handful of walnuts (optional)**
**3 eggs**
**⅔ cup (4 ½ oz/140 g) sugar**
**⅔ cup (3 ½ oz/100 g) whole-wheat flour**
**¾ cup (3 ½ oz/100 g) chestnut flour**
**½ Tbsp baking powder**
**pinch of salt**

Preheat the oven to 350°F (180°C). Butter and flour a cake pan.

Melt the butter in the microwave or in a bowl set over a pan of simmering water. Quarter the figs. Coarsely chop the chestnuts.

Beat together the eggs and sugar in a large mixing bowl until light, fluffy, and doubled in volume. Gradually add the flours, salt, and melted butter. Using a wooden spoon, fold in three-quarters of the figs, all the chestnuts and walnuts, taking care not to crush them. Gently fold in the baking powder.

Transfer to the prepared pan, arrange the remaining figs on top and bake for about 40 minutes. Let cool in the pan slightly before turning out.

Tip  You can also add a pinch of ground cinnamon.

## PEAR AND ANISEED CAKE

Preparation time: 15 minutes
Cooking time: 40 minutes

2 pears
3 eggs
1 cup (5 oz/150 g) light brown sugar
1½ cups (6 oz/175 g) flour
10 Tbsp (5 oz/150 g) butter
½ tsp ground aniseed
½ Tbsp baking powder
pinch of salt

Preheat the oven to 350°F (180°C). Butter and flour a cake pan.

Melt the butter in a microwave or in a bowl set over a pan of simmering water and set aside.

Cut the pears into small pieces; do not peel.

Beat together the eggs and sugar in a large mixing bowl until light, fluffy, and doubled in volume. Gradually add the flour, salt, and melted butter. Using a wooden spoon, fold in the pears and aniseed. Gently fold in the baking powder.

Transfer to the prepared pan and bake for about 40 minutes. Let cool in the pan slightly before turning out.

## APPLE, CARROT, AND ALMOND CAKE

Preparation time: 20 minutes
Cooking time: 40 minutes

1 apple
1 carrot
8 Tbsp (¼ lb/125 g) butter
3 eggs
1 cup (5 oz/150 g) raw sugar
1¼ cups (5 oz/150 g) flour
1 cup (3½ oz/100 g) ground almonds
handful of raisins
2 tsp almond extract
zest and juice of 1 lemon
½ Tbsp baking powder
½ tsp baking soda
pinch of salt

Preheat the oven to 350°F (180°C). Butter and flour a cake pan.

Peel the apples and the carrots then grate finely. Melt the butter in a microwave or in a bowl set over a pan of simmering water.

Beat together the eggs and sugar in a large mixing bowl until light, fluffy, and doubled in volume. Gradually add the flour, salt, ground almonds, and melted butter. Using a wooden spoon, fold in the apples, carrots, raisins, almond extract, lemon zest and juice. Gently fold in the baking powder and baking soda.

Transfer to the prepared pan and bake for about 40 minutes. Let cool in the pan slightly before turning out.

## APPLE, RAISIN, AND WALNUT CAKE

Preparation time: 20 minutes
Cooking time: 40 minutes

10 Tbsp (5 oz/150 g) butter
2–3 apples (about 7 oz/200 g)
3 eggs
¾ cup + 2 Tbsp (6 oz/175 g) sugar
1½ cups (6 oz/175 g) flour
2 handfuls of raisins
handful of walnuts, chopped
½ tsp ground cinnamon
½ Tbsp baking powder
½ tsp baking soda
pinch of salt

Preheat the oven to 350°F (180°C). Butter and flour a cake pan.

Melt the butter in a microwave or in a bowl set over a pan of simmering water. Grate the apples; the easiest way is to quarter and core them first then grate from the inside toward the peel.

Beat together the eggs and sugar in a large mixing bowl until light, fluffy, and doubled in volume. Gradually add the flour, salt, and melted butter. Using a wooden spoon, fold in the apples, raisins, walnuts, and cinnamon. Gently fold in the baking powder and baking soda.

Transfer to the prepared pan and bake for about 40 minutes. Let cool in the pan slightly before turning out.

Variation  For a chocolate version of this cake, add 2 Tbsp unsweetened cocoa powder when adding the flour.

## PUMPKIN AND CLOVE CAKE

Preparation time: 20 minutes
Cooking time: 40 minutes

3½ oz (100 g) pumpkin
1 apple
3 eggs
¾ cup + 2 Tbsp (6 oz/175 g) sugar
6 Tbsp (3½ fl oz/100 mL) vegetable oil
¾ cup (3½ oz/100 g) flour
1 cup (3½ oz/100 g) ground almonds
handful of raisins
¼ tsp ground cloves
½ Tbsp baking powder
½ tsp baking soda
pinch of salt

Preheat the oven to 350°F (180°C). Butter and flour a cake pan.

Grate the pumpkin and the apple. If you do not have ground cloves, crush 5 whole cloves in a mortar and pestle.

Beat the eggs, sugar, and oil in a large mixing bowl. Gradually add the flour, ground almonds, salt, pumpkin, apple, raisins, and cloves. Stir until just combined without overmixing. Gently fold in the baking powder and baking soda.

Transfer to the prepared pan and bake for 40 minutes. Let cool in the pan slightly before turning out.

Variation  Add a handful of chopped pecans.

## MANGO VANILLA CAKE

Preparation time: 15 minutes
Cooking time: 40 minutes

10 Tbsp (5 oz/150 g) butter
1 mango
1 vanilla bean
3 eggs
¾ cup (5½ oz/160 g) sugar
1½ cups (6 oz/175 g) flour
½ Tbsp baking powder
pinch of salt

Preheat the oven to 350°F (180°C). Butter and flour a cake pan.

Melt the butter in a microwave or in a bowl set over a pan of simmering water. Peel the mango and cut the flesh off the pit into small pieces. With the tip of a small knife, split the vanilla bean and scrape the seeds into a mixing bowl.

Add the eggs and sugar to the vanilla seeds and beat until frothy. Gradually add the flour, melted butter, and salt. Using a wooden spoon, fold in the mango. Gently fold in the baking powder.

Transfer to the prepared pan and bake for 40 minutes. Let cool in the pan slightly before turning out.

## CARROT AND WALNUT CAKE

Preparation time: 20 minutes

2–3 (½ lb/250 g) carrots
2 handfuls of walnuts
2 eggs
⅔ cup (¼ lb/125 g) brown sugar
1¾ cups (7 oz/200 g) flour
8 Tbsp (¼ lb/125 g) butter
½ tsp ground cinnamon
½ Tbsp baking powder
½ tsp baking soda
pinch of salt

Preheat the oven to 350°F (180°C). Butter and flour a cake pan.

Peel the carrots and grate finely. Coarsely chop the walnuts. Melt the butter in a microwave or in a bowl set over a pan of simmering water and set aside.

Beat together the eggs and sugar in a large mixing bowl until light, fluffy, and doubled in volume. Gradually add the flour, melted butter, and salt. Using a wooden spoon, fold in the carrot, walnuts, and cinnamon. Gently fold in the baking powder and baking soda.

Transfer to the prepared pan and bake for 40 minutes. Let cool in the pan slightly before turning out.

Tip  This cake goes well with lemon icing (see page 96).

## APPLE AND ZUCCHINI CAKE

Preparation time: 20 minutes
Cooking time: 40 minutes

**3½ oz (100 g) apple**
**3½ oz (100 g) zucchini**
**2 oz (60 g) dark chocolate**
**3 eggs**
**1¼ cups (6 oz/175 g) light brown sugar**
**6 Tbsp (3½ fl oz/100 mL) vegetable oil**
**2 Tbsp unsweetened cocoa powder**
**1¾ cups (7 oz/200 g) flour**
**handful of walnuts, chopped**
**½ Tbsp baking powder**
**½ tsp baking soda**
**pinch of salt**

Preheat the oven to 350°F (180°C). Butter and flour a cake pan.

Coarsely grate the apple. Finely grate the zucchini. Break the chocolate into small pieces. The best way to do this is in a food processor, or with a mortar and pestle.

Beat the eggs, sugar, and oil in a large mixing bowl. Gradually add the cocoa powder, flour, salt, zucchini, apple, chocolate pieces, and walnuts. Stir until just combined without overmixing. Gently fold in the baking powder and baking soda.

Transfer to the prepared pan and bake for 40 minutes. Let cool in the pan slightly before turning out.

Note  The zucchini make this cake particularly moist; be sure to choose small, firm zucchini and these will give the finished cake the best texture.

A SPECIAL SECTION ON CHOCOLATE! DARK,
WHITE, OR COCOA POWDER… IT'S UP TO YOU
TO DECIDE.

# CHOCOLATE, BASIL, AND PEPPER CAKE

Preparation time: 20 minutes
Cooking time: 40 minutes

**3½ oz (100 g) dark chocolate**
**10 Tbsp (5 oz/150 g) butter**
**½ tsp Sichuan peppercorns**
**handful of fresh basil leaves**
**3 eggs**
**¾ cup + 2 Tbsp (6 oz/175 g) sugar**
**1½ cups (6 oz/175 g) flour**
**2 tsp unsweetened cocoa powder**
**3 Tbsp low-fat milk**
**½ Tbsp baking powder**
**½ tsp baking soda**
**pinch of salt**

Preheat the oven to 350°F (180°C). Butter and flour
a cake pan.

Melt the chocolate and the butter in a microwave
or in a bowl set over a pan of simmering water and
set aside. Grind the peppercorns to a powder with
a mortar and pestle. Finely chop the basil.

Beat together the eggs and sugar in a large mixing
bowl until light, fluffy, and doubled in volume.
Gradually add the flour, salt, the melted butter, and
chocolate. Add the cocoa powder, milk, basil, and
pepper. Using a wooden spoon, stir until just
combined without overmixing. Gently fold in the
baking powder and baking soda.

Transfer to the prepared pan and bake for about
40 minutes. Let cool in the pan slightly before
turning out.

Note  The pepper enhances the intensity of the chocolate
and the basil brings a touch of the unexpected.

## CHOCOLATE AND ORANGE PEEL CAKE

Preparation time: 15 minutes
Cooking time: 40 minutes

3½ oz (100 g) dark chocolate
10 Tbsp (5 oz/150 g) butter
5 oz (150 g) candied orange peel
3 eggs
¾ cup + 2 Tbsp (6 oz/175 g) sugar
1½ cups (6 oz/175 g) flour
2 Tbsp unsweetened cocoa powder
3 Tbsp low-fat milk
2 Tbsp sesame seeds
½ Tbsp baking powder
½ tsp baking soda (optional)
pinch of salt

Preheat the oven to 350°F (180°C). Butter and flour a cake pan.

Melt the chocolate and the butter in a microwave or in a bowl set over a pan of simmering water and set aside. Coarsely chop the orange peel, either by hand or in a food processor.

Beat together the eggs and sugar in a large mixing bowl until light, fluffy, and doubled in volume. Gradually add the flour, melted butter and chocolate, and salt. Add the cocoa powder, milk, orange peel, and sesame seeds. Using a wooden spoon, stir until just combined without overmixing. Gently fold in the baking powder and baking soda.

Transfer to the prepared pan and bake for about 40 minutes. Let cool in the pan slightly before turning out.

Note  The cocoa powder makes this cake deliciously dark and richer in taste and the milk keeps the texture from becoming too dense.

## IRISH WHISKEY CAKE

Preparation time: 20 minutes
Cooking time: 40 minutes

3½ oz (100 g) dark chocolate
10 Tbsp (5 oz/150 g) butter
3 eggs
¾ cup + 2 Tbsp (6 oz/175 g) sugar
1½ cups (6 oz/175 g) flour
2 tsp unsweetened cocoa powder
¼ cup (2 fl oz/60 mL) Irish cream liqueur (Baileys)
3 Tbsp whiskey
½ Tbsp baking powder
½ tsp baking soda
pinch of salt

Preheat the oven to 350°F (180°C). Butter and flour a cake pan.

Melt the chocolate and the butter in a microwave or in a bowl set over a pan of simmering water and set aside.

Beat together the eggs and sugar in a large mixing bowl until light, fluffy, and doubled in volume. Gradually add the flour, salt, and melted butter and chocolate. Add the cocoa powder and alcohols. Using a wooden spoon, stir until just combined without overmixing. Gently fold in the baking powder and baking soda.

Transfer to the prepared pan and bake for about 40 minutes. Let cool in the pan slightly before turning out.

Note  You can use all whiskey instead of Irish cream liqueur. Alternatively, if you really enjoy this liqueur, prepare the cake in individual pans. Before serving, scoop out a well in the middle of each cake and fill with extra Irish cream liqueur. Serve immediately!

## DOUBLE CHOCOLATE CAKE

Preparation time: 20 minutes
Cooking time: 40 minutes

3½ oz (100 g) dark chocolate
3½ oz (100 g) white chocolate
10 Tbsp (5 oz/150 g) butter
3 eggs
¾ cup + 2 Tbsp (6 oz/175 g) sugar
1½ cups (6 oz/175 g) flour
2 tsp unsweetened cocoa powder
3 Tbsp low-fat milk
½ Tbsp baking powder
½ tsp baking soda
pinch of salt

Preheat the oven to 350°F (180°C). Butter and flour a cake pan.

Break the white chocolate into small pieces and set aside. Melt the dark chocolate and the butter in a microwave or in a bowl set over a pan of simmering water and set aside.

Beat together the eggs and sugar in a large mixing bowl until light, fluffy, and doubled in volume. Gradually add the flour, salt, and melted butter and chocolate. Add the cocoa powder and milk. Using a wooden spoon, stir until just combined without overmixing. Gently fold in the baking powder and baking soda.

Transfer to the prepared pan, bury the white chocolate pieces in the batter and bake for about 40 minutes. Let cool in the pan slightly before turning out.

## CHOCOLATE CHIP AND PEAR CAKE

Preparation time: 20 minutes
Cooking time: 40 minutes

**2 cups (½ lb/250 g) flour**
**2 handfuls of walnuts (about 2 oz/60 g)**
**3½ oz (100 g) dried pears**
**3 Tbsp calvados (apple brandy)**
**1 egg**
**¾ cup + 2 Tbsp (6 oz/175 g) light brown sugar**
**¾ cup (7 fl oz/200 mL) buttermilk**
**6 Tbsp (3½ fl oz/100 mL) vegetable oil**
**3½ oz (100 g) chocolate chips**
**pinch of ground cinnamon**
**½ Tbsp baking powder**
**½ tsp baking soda**
**pinch of salt**

Preheat the oven to 350°F (180°C). Butter and flour a cake pan.

Roughly chop the walnuts and the pears. Soak the pears in the calvados while you prepare the cake batter.

Lightly beat the egg with the sugar, milk, and oil in a large mixing bowl. Gradually add in the flour, salt, cinnamon, nuts, and pears with the calvados. Using a wooden spoon, stir until just combined without overmixing. Gently fold in the baking powder and baking soda.

Transfer to the prepared pan and bake for about 40 minutes. Let cool in the pan slightly before turning out.

Note  You can use regular milk acidulated with a few drops of lemon juice instead of the buttermilk.

TWO COLORS SWIRLING IN PERFECT HARMONY.
WHAT MORE CAN I SAY?

# GREEN TEA AND
# WHITE CHOCOLATE CAKE

Preparation time: 15 minutes
Cooking time: 40 minutes

10 Tbsp (5 oz/150 g) butter
2½ oz (75 g) white chocolate
3 eggs
¾ cup + 2 Tbsp (6 oz/175 g) sugar
¾ cup (3½ oz/100 g) flour
¾ cup (2½ oz/75 g) ground almonds
3 tsp green tea
½ Tbsp baking powder
½ tsp baking soda
pinch of salt

Preheat the oven to 350°F (180°C). Butter and flour a cake pan.

Melt the butter in a microwave or in a bowl set over a pan of simmering water and set aside. Melt the white chocolate separately and set aside.

Beat together the eggs and sugar in a large mixing bowl until light, fluffy, and doubled in volume. Gradually add the flour, ground almonds, melted butter, and salt. Gently fold in the baking powder and baking soda.

Divide the batter into two equal portions. Fold the green tea into one portion, and fold the white chocolate into the other.

Transfer to the prepared pan, pouring in the batters alternately. Use a fork to swirl the batters for a marbled effect. Bake for about 40 minutes. Let cool in the pan slightly before turning out.

# STRIPY CHOCOLATE ALMOND CAKE

Preparation time: 20 minutes
Cooking time: 40 minutes

10 Tbsp (5 oz/150 g) butter
2½ oz (75 g) dark chocolate
3 eggs
¾ cup + 2 Tbsp (6 oz/175 g) sugar
1½ cups (6 oz/175 g) flour
½ Tbsp baking powder
½ tsp baking soda
2 Tbsp cocoa powder
3 Tbsp low-fat milk
2 oz (50 g) slivered almonds
pinch of salt

Preheat the oven to 350°F (180°C). Butter and flour a cake pan.

Melt the butter in a microwave or in a bowl set over a pan of simmering water and set aside. Coarsely grate the chocolate.

Beat together the eggs and sugar in a large mixing bowl until light, fluffy, and doubled in volume. Gradually add the flour, salt, and melted butter. Gently fold in the baking powder and baking soda.

Divide the batter into two equal portions. Dissolve the cocoa powder in the milk, then add to one of the portions with the grated chocolate and blend. Fold the almonds into the other.

Transfer to the prepared pan, pouring in the batters alternately. Use a fork to swirl the batters for a marbled effect. Bake for about 40 minutes (cover the pan with aluminum foil toward the end of baking to prevent burning). Let cool in the pan slightly before turning out.

Note You can also decorate the top of the cake with slivered almonds.

# PISTACHIO AND LEMON CAKE

Preparation time: 20 minutes
Cooking time: 40 minutes

3½ oz (100 g) shelled pistachios
10 Tbsp (5 oz/150 g) butter
3 eggs
¾ cup + 2 Tbsp (6 oz/175 g) sugar
⅔ cup (2½ oz/75 g) flour
zest of 1 untreated lemon
juice of 2 lemons
½ Tbsp baking powder
½ tsp baking soda
pinch of salt

Preheat the oven to 350°F (180°C). Butter and flour a cake pan.

Grind the pistachios to a powder using a food processor. Melt the butter in a microwave or in a bowl set over a pan of simmering water.

Beat together the eggs and sugar in a large mixing bowl until light, fluffy, and doubled in volume. Gradually add the flour, salt, melted butter, lemon zest, and juice. Gently fold in the baking powder and baking soda.

Divide the batter into two equal portions. Fold the pistachios into one portion.

Transfer to the prepared pan, pouring in the batters alternately. Use a fork to swirl the batters for a marbled effect. Bake for about 40 minutes. Let cool in the pan slightly before turning out.

LIGHT DOES NOT NECESSARILY MEAN LIGHT IN
TASTE. IT MEANS A BIT LESS SUGAR AND A BIT
LESS BUTTER, AND IN SOME CASES NO MILK
OR EGGS.

## FRESH FRUIT CAKE

Preparation time: 20 minutes
Cooking time: 50 minutes

**7 oz (200 g) mixed fresh fruit in season**
**(apricots, plums, pears, cherries, apples, peaches, etc)**
**2 eggs**
**⅔ cup (¼ lb/125 g) light brown sugar**
**2 pots (8 fl oz/230 g) set plain yogurt**
**⅓ cup (2¾ fl oz/80 mL) olive oil**
**1¾ cups (7 oz/200 g) flour**
**½ Tbsp baking powder**
**pinch of salt**

Preheat the oven to 350°F (180°C). Butter and flour
a cake pan.

Cut the fruit into pieces.

Beat the eggs, sugar, yogurt, and oil together
in a large mixing bowl. Gradually add the flour,
salt, and the fruit, reserving a few pieces for
decoration. Using a wooden spoon, stir until just
combined without overmixing. Gently fold in the
baking powder.

Transfer to the prepared pan, arrange the fruit on
top, and bake for about 50 minutes. Let cool in the
pan slightly before turning out.

Note  Almost any fresh fruit can be used in this recipe.

## RED BERRY CAKE

Preparation time: 20 minutes
Cooking time: 50 minutes

5 Tbsp (2½ oz/75 g) butter
3 eggs
½ cup (¼ lb/125 g) light brown sugar
1 cup (3½ oz/100 g) whole-wheat flour
¾ cup (3½ oz/100 g) flour
1 pot (4 fl oz/115 g) set plain yogurt
10 oz (300 g) mixed red berries
½ Tbsp baking powder
pinch of salt

Preheat the oven to 350°F (180°C). Butter and flour a cake pan.

Melt the butter in a microwave or in a bowl set over a pan of simmering water and set aside.

Beat together the eggs and sugar in a large mixing bowl until light, fluffy, and doubled in volume. Gradually add the flours, salt, melted butter, and yogurt. Add the berries. Using a wooden spoon, stir until just combined without overmixing or crushing the fruit. Gently fold in the baking powder.

Transfer to the prepared pan and bake for about 50 minutes. Let cool in the pan slightly before turning out.

## BLUEBERRY AND LEMON CAKE

Preparation time: 20 minutes
Cooking time: 50 minutes

7 oz (200 g) blueberries, fresh or frozen
3 eggs
¾ cup + 2 Tbsp (6 oz/175 g) sugar
2 cups (½ lb/250 g) flour
8 Tbsp (¼ lb/125 g) butter
zest and juice of 1 lemon
7 oz (200 g) quark or fromage frais or ricotta cheese
1 Tbsp baking powder
pinch of salt

Preheat the oven to 350°F (180°C). Butter and flour a cake pan.

Melt the butter in a microwave or in a bowl set over a pan of simmering water and set aside.

If you are using frozen blueberries, defrost them first but do not let them become too soft, otherwise they will reduce to a purée when you mix them into the batter.

Beat together the eggs and sugar in a large mixing bowl until light, fluffy, and doubled in volume. Gradually add the flour, salt, melted butter, the lemon zest and juice, and the fromage frais. Stir in the blueberries, taking care not to crush them. Gently fold in the baking powder.

Transfer to the prepared pan and bake for 50 minutes. Let cool in the pan slightly before turning out.

Tip  If you are using frozen blueberries, allow them to defrost completely. Check that they are still firm; if not, reduce them to a purée before combining in the batter.

## REDCURRANT CAKE

Preparation time: 20 minutes
Cooking time: 40 minutes

3½ oz (100 g) candied orange peel
5 oz (150 g) redcurrants, fresh or frozen
2 eggs
¾ cup (5 oz/150 g) light brown sugar
¾ cup (7 fl oz/200 mL) buttermilk
6 Tbsp (3½ fl oz/100 mL) vegetable oil
1½ cups (7 oz/200 g) flour
¾ cup (3½ oz/100 g) rolled oats
pinch of ground cinnamon
½ Tbsp baking powder
pinch of salt

Preheat the oven to 350°F (180°C). Butter and flour a cake pan.

Chop the orange peel coarsely. Wash and strip the redcurrants from their stems. If you are using frozen fruit, defrost them first but do not let them become too soft, otherwise they will reduce to a purée when you mix them into the batter.

In a mixing bowl, beat together the eggs, sugar, milk, and oil. Gradually add the flour, oats, salt, chopped orange peel, redcurrants, and cinnamon. Stir carefully without overmixing. Gently fold in the baking powder.

Transfer to the prepared pan and bake for about 40 minutes. Let cool in the pan slightly before turning out.

Variation  Use cranberries instead of redcurrants.

## VERY LIGHT CAKE

Preparation time: 20 minutes
Cooking time: 50 minutes

**5 oz (150 g) mixed best-quality candied fruit**
**handful of shelled walnuts**
**2 Tbsp (1 oz/30 g) butter**
**5 egg whites**
**⅔ cup (4½ oz/140 g) sugar**
**⅔ cup (2½ oz/75 g) flour**
**½ Tbsp baking powder**
**pinch of salt**

Preheat the oven to 350°F (180°C). Butter and flour a cake pan.

Cut the candied fruit into a fine dice. Coarsely chop the walnuts. Melt the butter in a microwave or in a bowl set over a pan of simmering water.

In a mixing bowl, whisk the egg whites with a pinch of salt until they form stiff peaks. Continue beating, gradually adding in the sugar, until they are very firm and glossy.

Add the melted butter, flour, walnuts, and candied fruit. Gently fold in the baking powder.

Transfer to the prepared pan and bake for 50 minutes. Let cool slightly before turning out.

## PINEAPPLE CAKE

Preparation time: 20 minutes
Cooking time: 40 minutes

¼ prepared pineapple, fresh or frozen
2 eggs
¾ cup (6 oz/175 g) sugar
¾ cup (7 fl oz/200 mL) buttermilk
6 Tbsp (3½ fl oz/100 mL) olive oil
1¼ cups (7 oz/200 g) flour
¾ cup (3½ oz/100 g) rolled oats
pinch of ground cinnamon
½ Tbsp baking powder
pinch of salt

Preheat the oven to 350°F (180°C). Butter and flour a cake pan.

Cut the pineapple into pieces. If you are using frozen fruit, defrost the pieces first but do not let them become too soft, otherwise they will reduce to a purée when you mix them into the batter.

Beat the eggs, sugar, milk, and oil together in a large mixing bowl. Gradually add the flour, oats, salt, chopped pineapple (reserve a few pieces for decoration), and the cinnamon. Stir carefully without overmixing. Gently fold in the baking powder.

Transfer to the prepared pan, top with the reserved pineapple pieces and bake for about 40 minutes. Let cool in the pan slightly before turning out.

Note  You can use canned pineapple (1 x 8 oz/225 g can) in place of the fresh or frozen.

## ORCHARD FRUIT CAKE

Preparation time: 20 minutes
Cooking time: 50 minutes

7 oz (200 g) fresh fruit (peaches, apricots, apples, pears)
handful of walnuts
2 eggs
¾ cup (5 oz/150 g) sugar
¾ cup (7 fl oz/200 mL) buttermilk
6 Tbsp (3½ fl oz/100 mL) vegetable oil
1¼ cups (7 oz/200 g) spelt flour
¾ cup (3½ oz/100 g) rolled oats
¼ tsp ground cinnamon
¼ tsp ground ginger
½ Tbsp baking powder
pinch of salt

Preheat the oven to 350°F (180°C). Butter and flour a cake pan.

Cut the fruit into pieces and coarsely chop the walnuts.

Whisk the eggs, sugar, milk, and oil together in a large mixing bowl. Add the flour, oats, and salt. Add the walnuts, cinnamon, ginger, and the fruit, reserving some pieces for decoration. Stir until just combined without overmixing. Gently fold in the baking powder.

Transfer to the prepared pan, arrange the reserved fruit on top, and bake for about 50 minutes. Let cool in the pan slightly before turning out.

## PEAR AND GINGER CAKE

Preparation time: 20 minutes
Cooking time: 40 minutes

1 large pear, or 2 small ones
2 eggs
¾ cup (5 oz/150 g) sugar
¾ cup (7 fl oz/200 mL) buttermilk
6 Tbsp (3½ fl oz/100 mL) olive oil
1¼ cups (7 oz/200 g) flour
¾ cup (3½ oz/100 g) rolled oats
½ tsp ground ginger
½ tsp turmeric
½ Tbsp baking powder
pinch of salt

Preheat the oven to 350°F (180°C). Butter and flour a cake pan.

Cut the pear into small pieces; do not peel.

Whisk the eggs, sugar, milk, and oil together in a large mixing bowl. Add the flour, oats, salt, ginger, turmeric, and pear. Blend with a wooden spoon until just combined without overmixing. Gently fold in the baking powder.

Transfer to the prepared pan and bake for about 40 minutes. Let cool in the pan slightly before turning out.

IN THIS SECTION, WE USE EVERYTHING THAT'S
IN YOUR CUPBOARD FOR THOSE FINISHING
TOUCHES: HONEY, PRESERVES, INSTANT
COFFEE, HERBS, A PINCH OF CINNAMON,
A HANDFUL OF SLIVERED ALMONDS… ANYTHING,
AND EVERYTHING, GOES!

## ORANGE MARMALADE CAKE

Preparation time: 20 minutes
Cooking time: 50 minutes

**10 Tbsp (5 oz/150 g) butter**
**handful of walnuts**
**3 eggs**
**⅔ cup (3½ oz/100 g) brown sugar**
**1½ cups (6 oz/175 g) flour or spelt flour**
**4 Tbsp orange marmalade**
**½ Tbsp baking powder**
**pinch of salt**

Preheat the oven to 350°F (180°C). Butter and flour
a cake pan.

Melt the butter in a microwave or in a bowl set
over a pan of simmering water. Coarsely chop the
walnuts.

Whisk together the eggs and sugar in a large
mixing bowl until light, frothy, and doubled in
volume. Add the flour, salt, melted butter, and
walnuts. Add the marmalade and stir until just
combined without overmixing. Gently fold in the
baking powder.

Transfer to the prepared pan and bake for about
50 minutes. Let cool in the pan slightly before
turning out.

## ROSEMARY CAKE

Preparation time: 15 minutes
Cooking time: 40 minutes

**3 sprigs rosemary**
**3 eggs**
**¾ cup + 2 Tbsp (6 oz/175 g) sugar**
**½ cup (4 fl oz/125 mL) olive oil**
**¾ cup (3½ oz/100 g) whole-wheat flour**
**¾ cup (3½ oz/100 g) flour**
**½ Tbsp baking powder**
**pinch of salt**

Preheat the oven to 350°F (180°C). Butter and flour
a cake pan.

Strip the rosemary leaves from the stems and
chop coarsely.

Whisk together the eggs, sugar, and oil in a large
mixing bowl. Gradually add the flours, rosemary, and
salt. Stir until just combined without overmixing.
Gently fold in the baking powder.

Transfer to the prepared pan and bake for about
40 minutes. Let cool in the pan slightly before
turning out.

## TURMERIC POUND CAKE

Preparation time: 15 minutes
Cooking time: 40 minutes

**12 Tbsp (6 oz/175g) butter**
**3 eggs**
**¾ cup + 2 Tbsp (6 oz/175 g) sugar**
**1½ cups (6 oz/175 g) flour**
**1 tsp turmeric**
**juice of 2 lemons**
**zest of 1 untreated lemon**
**½ Tbsp baking powder**
**pinch of salt**

Preheat the oven to 350°F (180°C). Butter and flour
a cake pan.

Melt the butter in a microwave or in a bowl set
over a pan of simmering water.

Beat together the eggs and sugar in a large mixing
bowl until light, frothy, and doubled in volume.
Gradually add the flour, salt, and melted butter.
Stir in the turmeric, lemon juice, and zest. Gently
fold in the baking powder.

Transfer to the prepared pan and bake for about
40 minutes. Let cool in the pan slightly before
turning out.

## HONEY, LEMON, AND THYME CAKE

Preparation time: 20 minutes
Cooking time: 50 minutes

**4 Tbsp (2 oz/60 g) butter**
**handful of fresh thyme (or rosemary or basil)**
**3 eggs**
**¼ cup (2 oz/60 g) sugar**
**3 heaping Tbsp (¼ lb/125 g) honey**
**2 cups (½ lb/250 g) flour**
**juice of 2 lemons**
**zest of 1 untreated lemon**
**½ Tbsp baking powder**
**½ tsp baking soda**
**pinch of salt**

Preheat the oven to 350°F (180°C). Butter and flour a cake pan.

Melt the butter in a microwave or in a bowl set over a pan of simmering water. Finely chop the thyme.

Beat together the eggs, sugar, and honey in a large mixing bowl until light, frothy, and doubled in volume. Gradually add the flour, salt, melted butter, lemon juice, and zest. Add the thyme. Gently fold in the baking powder and baking soda.

Transfer to the prepared pan and bake for about 50 minutes. Let cool in the pan slightly before turning out.

## TWO COFFEE CAKE

Preparation time: 15 minutes
Cooking time: 50 minutes

**10 Tbsp (5 oz/150 g) butter**
**3 eggs**
**¾ cup + 2 Tbsp (6 oz/175 g) sugar**
**1½ cups (6 oz/175 g) flour**
**3 Tbsp instant coffee**
**1 Tbsp ground coffee**
**zest of 1 untreated orange**
**½ Tbsp baking powder**
**pinch of salt**

Preheat the oven to 350°F (180°C). Butter and flour a cake pan.

Melt the butter in a microwave or in a bowl set over a pan of simmering water.

Beat together the eggs and sugar in a large mixing bowl until light, frothy, and doubled in volume. Gradually add the flour, salt, and melted butter. Add the orange zest and the coffees. Stir until just combined without overmixing. Gently fold in the baking powder.

Transfer to the prepared pan and bake for about 50 minutes. Let cool in the pan slightly before turning out.

## ALMOND CHICORY CAKE

Preparation time: 15 minutes
Cooking time: 50 minutes

**10 Tbsp (5 oz/150 g) butter**
**3 eggs**
**¾ cup + 2 Tbsp (6 oz/175 g) sugar**
**¾ cup (3½ oz/100 g) flour**
**1 cup (3½ oz/100 g) ground almonds**
**1 handful (about 2 oz/60 g) slivered almonds**
**3 Tbsp instant chicory (available in healthfood stores)**
**½ Tbsp baking powder**
**pinch of salt**

Preheat the oven to 350°F (180°C). Butter and flour a cake pan.

Melt the butter in a microwave or in a bowl set over a pan of simmering water.

Beat the eggs and sugar together in a large mixing bowl until light, frothy, and doubled in volume. Gradually add the flour, salt, ground almonds, melted butter, three-quarters of the slivered almonds, and the chicory. Gently fold in the baking powder.

Transfer to the prepared pan, arrange the remaining slivered almonds on top, and bake for about 50 minutes. Let cool in the pan slightly before turning out.

Note  To prevent the slivered almonds from turning too dark, cover with aluminum foil after 15 minutes of baking.

## ANISE CAKE

Preparation time: 15 minutes
Cooking time: 50 minutes

**10 Tbsp (5 oz/150 g) butter**
**3 eggs**
**¾ cup + 2 Tbsp (6 oz/175 g) sugar**
**2 cups (½ lb/250 g) flour**
**2 fl oz (60 mL) pastis**
**1 tsp ground aniseed**
**½ Tbsp baking powder**
**pinch of salt**

Preheat the oven to 350°F (180°C). Butter and flour a cake pan.

Melt the butter in a microwave or in a bowl set over a pan of simmering water.

Beat the eggs and sugar together in a large mixing bowl until light, frothy, and doubled in volume. Gradually add the flour, salt, melted butter, pastis, and the aniseed. Gently fold in the baking powder.

Transfer to the prepared pan and bake for about 50 minutes. Let cool in the pan slightly before turning out.

INDICES

# INDEX OF RECIPES

# INDEX

# ADDRESS BOOK

AU FIL DES COULEURS
31, rue de l'Abbé Grégoire 75006, France (01 45 44 74 00)
BHV
52, rue de Rivoli 75004, France (01 42 74 90 00)
DESIGNER'S GUILD
10, rue St Nicolas 75012, France 501 44 67 80 70)
FLAMANT HOME INTÉRIORS
8, rue de Furstenberg 75006, France (01 56 81 12 40)
HABITAT
0800 010 800
HOME AUTOUR DU MONDE
8, rue des Francs Bourgeois 75003, France (01 42 77 06 08)
IKEA
www.ikea.com
ISKANDAR
10, rue de l'Abbaye 75006, France (01 43 25 18 20)
LE BON MARCHÉ RIVE GAUCHE
24, rue de Sèvres 75007, France (01 44 39 80 30)
MONOPRIX
www.monoprix.fr

Translation: JMS Books LLP; jackie@moseleystrachan.com
Layout: cb design

Text © Marabout 2006
Photography © Marabout

Editor: Natacha Kotchetkova
Design: emigreen.com
Proofreader: Véronique Dussidour

This edition published in North America in 2008 by Whitecap Books Ltd.
For more information, contact Whitecap Books, 351 Lynn Avenue,
North Vancouver, British Columbia, Canada V7J 2C4. Visit our website
at www.whitecap.ca.

ISBN 10: 1-55285-954-1
ISBN 13: 978-1-55285-954-4

Printed in China